Professional Pilot's Study Guide
Volume 5

Hydraulics

Professional Pilot's Study Guide Volume 5

Hydraulics

Mike Burton

Airlife
England

Copyright © 1992 Mike Burton

First published in the UK in 1992
by Airlife Publishing Ltd

British Library Cataloguing in Publication Data
A catalogue record of this book is available from the British Library

ISBN 1 85310 277 6

Printed in England by Livesey Ltd, Shrewsbury SY3 9EB

Airlife Publishing Ltd

101 Longden Road, Shrewsbury SY3 9EB

Contents

1

GENERAL PRINCIPLES

1.1 Introduction

Hydraulic systems using fluid under pressure are extensively used to operate major aircraft services on modern civil aircraft. Such services as alighting gear, flaps, air brakes, wheel brakes and primary flying control surfaces, are operated by hydraulic systems and such systems must provide reliability and some form of emergency back up system in the event the main system should fail.

1.2 Advantages

Hydraulic systems have numerous advantages over their mechanical counterparts in that hydraulic systems can be designed to:

(a) Provide smooth and steady movement.

(b) Provide hydraulic power which is confined to pipelines and components, and therefore much of the strengthening of the aircraft structure is not required as is the case with mechanical systems.

(c) Provide greater transmission of power for weight of equipment.

(d) Simplify installation in that pipelines can be easily bent to go around obstructions.

(e) Provide variation in speed of operation without the use of gearing as would be required in a mechanical system.

(f) Easily obtain its power to drive pumps etc, from the aircraft engines.

(g) Relieve the pilot of effort to operate the cockpit controls by requiring minimal force to move the switches and levers to operate hydraulic controlled systems.

1.3 Hydraulic Fluid

Hydraulic fluids generally are developed to provide the following requirements:

(a) Be free flowing at all operating temperatures.

(b) Have low freezing and high boiling points.

(c) Not affect or be affected by the materials in the components.

(d) Have good lubrication qualities.

(e) Not deteriorate or form sludge.

(f) Have a high flash point.

1.4 Types of Hydraulic Fluid

There are various types of hydraulic fluid in use on current civil aircraft, the following are the most widely used:

(a) D.T.D. 585
This fluid is probably the most widely used, it is RED in colour, is mineral based, and systems using it require synthetic rubber seals to be fitted.

(b) Castor or Vegetable
This fluid is either castor or vegetable based, is yellow in colour, and requires systems to be fitted with natural rubber seals when it is used.

(c) Skydrol
This is a Phosphate Ester based fluid, which is blue in colour and requires special Butyl rubber seals when it is used in a system.

Note: Skydrol is sometimes considered to be purple/blue in colour.

1.5 All liquids generally have a high resistance to compression and when the liquid is subjected to pressure the reduction in its volume is very small; it is this fact which is responsible for the positive action which hydraulic actuation provides. As an example a pressure of approximately 5000lb per sq in would be needed to reduce the volume of a hydraulic fluid by one per cent, and if the same pressure was to be applied to air it would reduce the volume of the air to about 1/300th of its original volume. Whilst different hydraulic fluids possess different compression values for all practical purposes hydraulic fluid can be considered to be virtually incompressible. Fig.1-1 illustrates a comparison between hydraulic fluid and air when subjected to pressure.

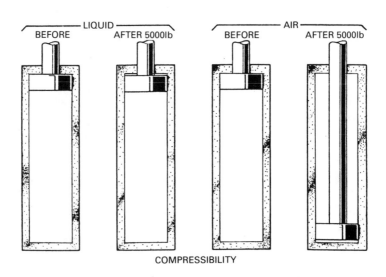

COMPRESSIBILITY

Fig.1-1. Comparison of Compressibility.

2

1.6 Fluid Pressure

Pressure is defined as force per unit area; for example pounds per square inch. Force is the total load acting upon a surface, in this example, expressed in pounds (lb). While pressure refers to the total force divided by the area upon which it is acting (lb per sq in or psi). Pressure obeys certain laws which state that 'if pressure is applied to a liquid in a confined space, that pressure will be felt equally in all directions without reduction throughout the liquid and will react at right angles to the surface of the container'. Fig.1-2 shows the principle of pressure on a surface.

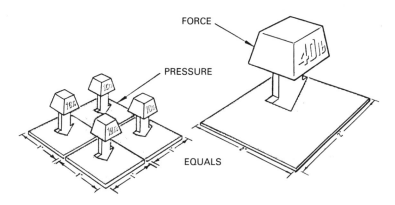

Fig.1-2. Pressure on a Surface.

1.7 Force as a result of Fluid Pressure

In paragraph 1.6 it has been stated that when pressure is generated in a confined space that fluid pressure will be transmitted equally in all directions. This principle can be used to great advantage in hydraulic systems, in that, if a force is applied to a fluid within a pipeline pressure is then generated. That pressure will be transmitted through the pipeline and by use of a jack or actuator the pressure can then be converted back into a mechanical force. Fig.1-3 shows an example of the use of hydraulic pressure and its conversion through a hydraulic jack to create mechanical force.

Such a principle may be used to operate such items of aircraft equipment as undercarriage units, flaps and wheel brakes. There is an almost endless list of components that can be operated in this way.

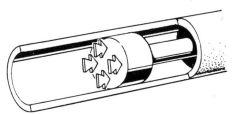

Fig.1-3. Force due to Fluid Pressure.

3

1.8 Differential Areas

Design of a hydraulic jack will vary according to the specific needs of the system. In some systems for a specific pressure value the same force is required in each direction of movement of the hydraulic jack. In other systems this is not an important requirement. As a result another aspect of force produced by fluid pressure must be examined, the effect of differential areas. For example examine Fig.1-4. At *A* in the Figure fluid is applied to the piston head end of the cylinder, under pressure, and the force exerted will move the piston to the left. If fluid is directed to the piston rod end of the piston, shown at *B*, the result will be the piston will move to the right. If the two end connections are coupled together, as shown at *C* and fluid pressure is applied to both ends simultaneously, the piston will not remain stationary, but will move to the left. This is due to an unbalanced force on the piston head equal to the pressure multiplied by the cross sectional area of the piston rod. A jack, or actuator so designed is termed a differential piston jack.

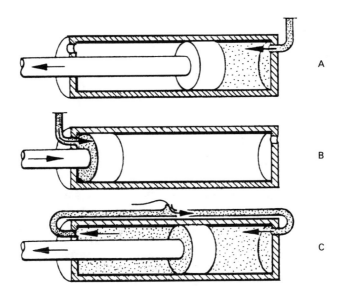

Fig.1-4. Differential Areas.

1.9 Equal Areas

Some systems require an ideal force to be applied to the piston in both directions. In order to achieve this a jack rod, or ram is attached to both sides of the piston establishing an equal surface piston area on both sides. Normally only one piston ram is used to actually operate the service, the other ram is used solely to establish the equal area piston. Such jacks, or actuators are commonly used to operate flaps and similar devices where the forces required must be balanced. The ram which is not used to operate the service is normally fitted with a spent travel tube, or housing. An example of an equal area jack is shown in Fig.1-5.

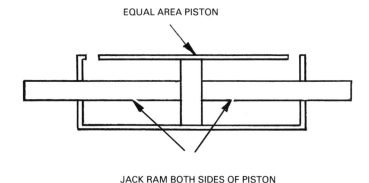

EQUAL AREA PISTON

JACK RAM BOTH SIDES OF PISTON

Fig.1-5. Equal Area Piston Jack.

1.10 Bramah's Press

It has been established that fluid pressure acts equally in all directions, also that the load that can be moved by a piston depends upon the pressure and the piston area. Consider a vessel containing a quantity of liquid, fitted with two open cylinders, each containing a piston which can slide within the cylinders. If the pistons have the same area and a force is applied to one piston, then, an additional force of equal magnitude must be applied to the other piston in order to maintain balance. See Fig.1-6.

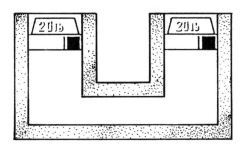

Fig.1-6. Bramah's Press Principle.

Now consider the situation that one piston has half the surface area of the other. To maintain balance, the force applied to the small piston must be half the force applied to the large piston. This fact was discovered by Joseph Bramah who invented a hydraulic press. He also stated that 'under a given load, the smaller the area it acts upon the greater the pressure produced', and 'the greater the area under pressure, the greater the force available'. See Fig.1-7.

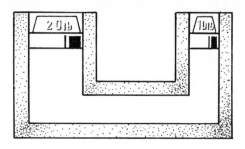

Fig.1-7.

1.11   Application of Bramah's Principle

Fig.1-8 illustrates the application of fluid pressure in a simple form of hydraulic machine. The area of one piston is 1 sq in and the other 2 sq in. A 10lb weight pushing down on the 1 sq in piston area will set up a pressure of 10 psi. This pressure is transmitted throughout the fluid, and on each sq in of the 2 sq in piston area there will be a force of 10lb. Therefore, disregarding the weight of the fluid, each square inch of the large piston will experience an upward force of 10lb so the 20lb weight placed on this piston will just maintain balance.

A very small weight added to the 10lb on the small piston will cause some of the fluid in the small cylinder to flow to the large cylinder and the large piston plus the 20lb weight will move in an upward direction. Bramah's press which worked on this principle, provided mechanical advantage. He used a large area piston on the 'load end', and a small area piston on the 'effort end', so that a small force lifted a heavy load.

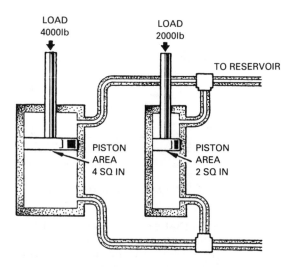

Fig.1-8. Application of Bramah's Press Principle.

It should be realised that the gain is offset by the greater distance through which the small piston will have to move, or push, than that through which the large piston is moved; also, that the speed of movement of the large piston will be less than that of the small piston.

In the aircraft hydraulic system Bramah's principle can be applied to the movement of different loads subject to one pressure. Fig.1-8 illustrates one pressure moving a large and a small piston under different loads. The pistons move at the same speed but if these conditions are changed, for instance, by the load on either piston being altered, or if the area of one piston is increased in relation to the area of the other piston, the speed, or rate of travel of the pistons will also change. However, in practice the pistons are not likely to move at the same speed since many other factors are also involved, such as friction between moving parts etc.

1.12 Fluid Flow through an Orifice

This information is of importance when understanding how a restrictor, or similar valve, performs. As can be seen in Fig.1-9 if you consider a horizontal pipe through which fluid is flowing, where at some section there is an orifice, then experiments have shown that a steady motion is set up in the fluid. These streamlines converge toward the orifice where the velocity of the fluid increases. After passing through the orifice the streamlines continue to converge until the point *B* is reached. This point is known as the 'Vena contracta', and at this point the fluid will expand outwards into the full diameter pipe. The orifice constitutes a sudden contraction of a pipe and will cause a loss of pressure due to the sudden contraction itself. The total reduction in pressure is not only due to the contraction but is also due to the sudden expansion after the vena contracta is reached.

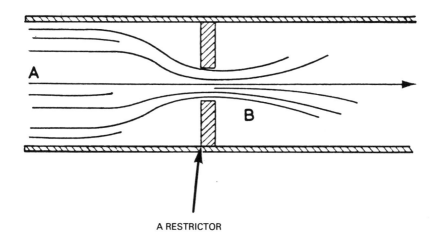

A RESTRICTOR

Fig.1-9. Fluid Flow through an Orifice.

1.13   The Heating Effect of Leakage

With a hydraulic shock absorber, the energy to be absorbed is first given to the fluid in the shock absorber and this fluid is forced through small orifices where the energy is converted into heat energy. In this case the heat effect is deliberate. Again in an aircraft hydraulic system when the pump has cut out it takes fluid from the reservoir and circulates it round a closed circuit. The fluid after leaving the pump is under pressure and hence has some energy. This energy is dissipated when the fluid reaches the reservoir and causes the reservoir temperature to rise. If there were no heat losses the temperature would rise indefinitely, but in practice the reservoir temperature settles down to a steady value. A leakage in the system will cause the fluid temperature to rise if it is an internal leak.

TEST YOURSELF 1
GENERAL PRINCIPLES

1. Hydraulic fluid should have a:
   - (a) low flash point.
   - (b) high freezing and low boiling point.
   - (c) high flash point.
   - (d) freezing point not lower than 0 degrees 'C'.

   Ref. 1.3.

2. D.T.D. 585 hydraulic fluid is coloured:
   - (a) blue.
   - (b) red.
   - (c) green.
   - (d) yellow.

   Ref. 1.4.

3. Castor based hydraulic fluids require:
   - (a) natural rubber seals.
   - (b) synthetic rubber seals.
   - (c) butyl rubber seals.
   - (d) leather seals.

   Ref. 1.4.

4. D.T.D. 585 hydraulic fluid requires:
   - (a) synthetic rubber seals.
   - (b) natural rubber seals.
   - (c) butyl rubber seals.
   - (d) leather seals.

   Ref. 1.4.

5. Skydrol hyradulic fluid is coloured:
   - (a) red.
   - (b) yellow.
   - (c) orange.
   - (d) blue.

   Ref. 1.4.

6. Hydraulic fluids:
   - (a) are incompressible.
   - (b) can be considered for practical purposes to be incompressible.

(c) are readily compressible.

(d) are only compressible over 100,000 psi.

Ref. 1.5.

7. Pressure in a hydraulic system:

(a) is defined as force per unit area.

(b) is defined as pressure per unit area.

(c) is defined as pressure felt in one directional axis only.

(d) is defined as force times area.

Ref. 1.6.

8. If 3000 psi is applied to a differential area jack at both connections at the same time.

(a) the force will be equal on both sides of the piston.

(b) the force will be greater on the ram side of the piston.

(c) the force will be greater on the opposite piston face to the ram.

(d) the piston will remain stationary.

Ref. 1.8.

9. D.T.D. 585 hydraulic fluid is:

(a) vegetable based.

(b) castor based.

(c) phosphate ester based.

(d) mineral based.

Ref. 1.4.

10. An equal area piston jack:

(a) is not used in aircraft hydraulic systems.

(b) is used in flap circuits.

(c) is used only in undercarriage circuits.

(d) will provide a balanced force when pressures are unbalanced.

Ref. 1.9.

2

A BASIC
HYDRAULIC SYSTEM

2.1 Introduction

In this chapter the basic principles discussed in chapter one are put into effect in the form of a basic hydraulic system which uses a number of essential components to produce a working system that could be used to operate a service.

2.2. Essential Components

In order for a hydraulic system to operate as a complete system to move a service in two directions, for example, undercarriage from down to up, and from the up to down positions, the following components must be used in the hydraulic system:

(a) Jack or Actuator

The Jack, or Actuator, as described in chapter one is the most widely used component to convert hydraulic pressure into mechanical energy and comprises of a cyclinder in which is fitted a piston and piston rod or ram. The piston is fitted with seals which prevent hydraulic fluid leaking from one side of the piston to the other. A normal jack has two pipe connections through which the hydraulic fluid is fed under pressure from a control valve. If it is assumed the circuit, or system in Fig.2-1 is operating an undercarriage, then when undercarriage down is selected fluid will enter the pipe connection at the left hand side of the jack and the pressure of the fluid will exert a force on the piston moving the undercarriage down by forcing the piston and jack ram to move to the right. The fluid to the right of the piston, which is not under high pressure generated by the pump, will be forced out of the jack cylinder by the piston moving to the right, this is termed return fluid, as it is forced through the pipelines and components back to the reservoir.

(b) Reservoir

The detailed construction and operation of the reservoir is explained in the following chapters, for the purpose of understanding the operation of the system shown in Fig.2-1 only a simple description is given.

The reservoir supplies a reserve of hydraulic fluid to compensate for minor leakages in the system and provides a storage space for the returning hydraulic fluid. When a selection is made at the control valve, fluid is drawn by the pump from the reservoir.

(c) Pump

A simple hand pump is shown in Fig.2-1 to explain the operation of this basic hydraulic system. Most larger hydraulic systems would have a pump driven by the aircraft engine and simply termed the Engine Driven Pump (EDP).

The hand pump draws fluid from the reservoir and directs it to the control valve. Dependent upon the selection of the control valve will depend upon which end of the jack the fluid is directed. The hand pump is normally designed to give a continuous flow of fluid, that fluid being used to convert, through the jack, the hydraulic pressure into mechanical energy. Most aircraft hand pumps are of a double acting type to ensure a continuous flow is provided.

(d) Control Valve

The control valve in a hydraulic system may be mechanically operated by the pilot, or electrically operated. Control valves take many forms, some of which will be discussed in later chapters. In the basic hydraulic system illustrated the control valve directs the fluid from the hydraulic pump to the end connection of the jack selected in order to move the jack in the desired direction. At the same time the control valve connects the returning fluid to the common return therefore controlling the displaced fluid at the same time.

Some control valves may also have a neutral selection which provides a facility to be able to stop the jack in any desired position.

(e) Conclusion

The simple system shown in Fig.2-1 contains the minimum essential components to make a basic hydraulic system work. Under normal circumstances additional valves will be required to perform other tasks within the system; these will be dealt with later.

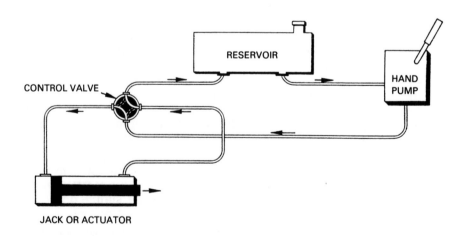

Fig.2-1. Basic Hydraulic System.

2.3 Hydraulic System Pressure

An important factor in the design of hydraulic systems is the pressure at which the system will operate. Since for a given work capacity higher system pressures imply lesser flows, coupled with a reduction in the size of all the components within the system there is a natural tendency towards the use of higher system pressures. The theoretical limitation to this trend is one of structure and the resulting increase of weight to all components within the system to provide greater strength in order to withstand the greater pressures. For a given load, as pressure increases, area decreases directly and diameter decreases as the square root. This decrease affects both piston and piston rod, and, or ram, in order to achieve the necessary resistance to the forces subjected to such components, the section of the piston rod may have to be greatly increased. Many installations require the jack to have a stroke/diameter ratio of 6:1 or 8:1 and even with a solid piston rod, the working pressure cannot exceed 5000-6000 psi for structural reasons.

Higher pressures therefore do not always result in jacks and other components of lighter weight, although the reduced bulk of components is often an advantage.

There are many factors which control the hydraulic system pressure that is selected and most current large commercial aircraft operate at system pressures between 3000 and 4000 psi. Some sub-systems within an aircraft hydraulic system may operate at a reduced pressure, this is common with wheel brake systems.

2.4 Constant Pressure or Constant Flow Systems

Earlier types of aircraft hydraulic systems tended to use what is called a constant flow system principle. In this type of system the pump, or pumps, delivered a constant flow rate of hydraulic fluid and pressure was determined entirely by the load requirements of the service that was connected to it. If two or more services were connected at the same time then that which required the lesser pressure would move first, in other words the pressure generated was dependent upon the resistance of the individual circuit. Overall system pressure was controlled by a pressure relief valve of some type. The pumps used in this type of system delivered a constant flow rate for a given engine rpm. Modern systems are based on the constant pressure principle which normally takes one of two forms. The first type is a constant flow, or constant volume pump, and the system pressure is controlled by a cut out valve aided by an accumulator, and the second type of system has a variable volume pump which controls system pressure from within the pump itself, both types will be discussed in detail in later chapters.

TEST YOURSELF 2
A BASIC HYDRAULIC SYSTEM

1. Hydraulic pressure is converted into mechanical energy by:
   - (a) a hydraulic pump.
   - (b) a hydraulic jack.
   - (c) the control valve.
   - (d) the reservoir.

   Ref. 2.2.

2. Return fluid from the jack is:
   - (a) returned direct to the reservoir.
   - (b) returned to the reservoir via the pump.
   - (c) returned to the reservoir via the control valve.
   - (d) returned to the reservoir via the pump and control valve.

   Ref. 2.2.

3. Aircraft hydraulic handpumps are normally:
   - (a) fitted after the control valve.
   - (b) in the return line between the control valve and reservoir.
   - (c) in the supply line between the reservoir and control valve.
   - (d) in the supply line between the control valve and jack.

   Ref. 2.2.

4. The reservoir supplies:
   - (a) a reserve of fluid to compensate for minor leaks.
   - (b) pressure to the pump.
   - (c) a means to store all the system fluid when it is not in use.
   - (d) a reserve of fluid should the system fail.

   Ref. 2.2.

5. The jack may be stopped at any position:
   - (a) by a control valve fitted with a neutral selection.
   - (b) by stopping the pump.
   - (c) by reversing the control valve.
   - (d) by stalling the jack.

   Ref. 2.2.

3

MAIN HYDRAULIC SUPPLY SYSTEMS

3.1 Introduction

The main, or primary, hydraulic supply systems on most modern medium and large aircraft are fitted with a minimum of two hydraulic engine driven pumps. They are usually so arranged that each pump is a back up to the other in the event one pump fails. Multi-pump systems will be explained in more detail later. For the purposes of clarity and ease of understanding a single pump supply system will be discussed in this chapter. The following is an example and not a specific system as fitted to a particular aircraft.

3.2 Hydraulic System Types

In general terms there are two main types of hydraulic supply system which are sometimes known by some authorities as:

(a) Self Idling.

(b) Non-Self Idling.

Modern hydraulic systems used on aircraft operate at a constant pressure and the above type names reflect on the ability of the pump to off load or idle when the system has reached maximum normal working pressure.

The Self Idling Type of system has a pump fitted which is capable of controlling the system pressure within the pump itself, hence the name Self Idling.

The Non-Self Idling system uses a pump which delivers a constant flow and requires another component to be fitted to the system to control the system pressure.

In the following paragraphs a supply system with each of the types of pump fitted will be examined.

3.3 Self Idling Type Supply System (Variable Volume)

This type of hydraulic supply system generally comprises the following components, some aircraft however, may require variations in the layout or components used. The following displays all the basic requirements that may be found in a supply system of this type.

(a) Reservoir

The design details of reservoirs are dealt with later in this volume. The reservoir is normally situated in the aircraft where ease of

15

access may be gained for servicing purposes, such as checking the fluid level, or topping it up. Wherever possible it is also positioned so it is above the level of the pump to ensure it has a head of pressure in order that it may provide a positive fluid supply to the pump. In situations where the reservoir cannot be located above the pump then the reservoir is pressurised in order to provide a head of pressure.

The reservoir must also be large enough to provide a reserve of fluid, to compensate for minor system leakages, allow for jack, or actuator, ram displacement, and the return fluid from the jacks or relief valves and other such components. In some systems the reservoir must also be large enough to ensure an adequate volume of fluid is maintained in the total system for temperature control purposes.

Under normal operating conditions, fluid is drawn from the reservoir by the engine driven pump via a filter.

(b) Low Pressure Filter

This filter, situated between the reservoir and engine driven pump, is sometimes known as a suction filter. It is situated at this point in the system to ensure that any foreign matter which has collected in the reservoir will be removed from the fluid before it enters the pump.

(c) Engine Driven Pump

All normal operational supply functions are provided by the engine driven pump which is driven by the aircraft engine, normally via a gearbox, and in a self idling system, or variable volume system, when a selection of a service is made the pump moves to the 'on load', or 'on stroke', position and starts to pump a flow of fluid to the selected service. In the example that flaps are selected 'down', when the flap actuators reach the end of their travel pressure will build up in the system, when the pressure reaches the system maximum normal working pressure a relief valve assembly within the pump, or similar device, will cause the pump to move to the idle mode and stop delivering further fluid to the flaps. The pump is lubricated by the system fluid that passes through it, for this reason when the pump is in the idle position a small amount of fluid is still passed through the engine driven pump for such lubrication purposes. As can be seen in Fig.3-1 this type of pump has three connections that is, the inlet from the reservoir, the outlet to the system, and the third connection, a pipeline back to the reservoir. On some older type pumps when the pump is not supplying a selected service and maximum normal working pressure has been reached, the pump continues to supply a full flow of fluid but that flow is directed back to the reservoir. On modern pumps however, the return line to the reservoir allows small quantities of fluid to be returned to the reservoir to maintain a constant temperature and viscosity within the pump.

(d) Ground Servicing Connections

As can be seen on Fig.3-1 ground servicing connections are provided in each of the pipelines to and from the engine driven pump. These are normally of a 'quick release' type and allow servicing functions to be carried out by connecting a ground, or external, source of hydraulic fluid flow from a type of servicing trolley.

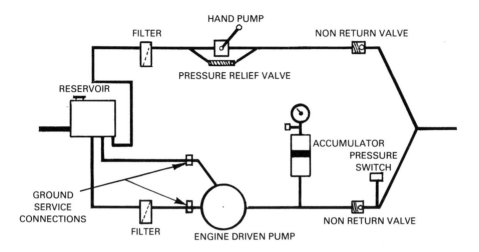

Fig.3-1. Self Idling Type Supply System (Variable Volume Pump).

(e) Non-Return Valves

As can be seen in Fig.3-1 a non-return valve, or check valve, is fitted after the engine driven pump. This is fitted to prevent fluid being pumped by the hand pump circuit flowing back through the engine driven pump instead of to the circuit.

(f) Pressure Switch

It is essential a warning device is fitted to the supply system to indicate to the pilot that a fault exists in the system. This normally takes the form of a warning light, usually coloured red, which illuminates when there is a reduction in hydraulic pressure below a certain value. The warning light is activated by a pressure switch which is usually located in the position indicated in Fig.3-1. On some aircraft an audible warning system is also provided and is also activated by the pressure switch.

(g) Hand Pump

On some aircraft a hand operated pump is provided for use in an emergency in the event the engine driven pump fails. In some cases the hand pump may also be provided with a separate supply of reserve fluid in order to operate some services in such circumstances. On most modern larger aircraft this type of emergency arrangement would be inadequate and so a second or standby engine driven pump is provided. Such emergency systems will be explained later. On most larger modern aircraft a hand pump is provided to assist with servicing operations and is normally a double acting type, that is to say, it provides a flow of fluid continuously as fluid is displaced by the action of the pump. Details of how this is achieved are given in the components chapter.

(h) Hand Pump Pressure Relief Valve
As with the engine driven pump the hand pump must not be allowed to overpressurise the system and so when maximum normal working pressure is reached the pump must be 'off loaded'. In the engine driven pump, the variable volume type, the pump is moved to an idle mode. In the case of the hand pump a pressure relief valve is provided to allow the pump to idle when maximum pressure is reached as shown in Fig.3-1. The pressure relief valve is usually fitted within the hand pump assembly itself, it is shown in Fig.3-1 as a separate component for simplicity.

(i) Hand Pump Non-Return Valve
A non-return valve, or check valve, is also fitted after the hand pump to prevent fluid from the engine driven pump passing back through the hand pump.

(j) Hand Pump Filter
A simple low pressure suction filter is fitted between the reservoir and the hand pump to provide clean fluid to the system.

3.4 Non Self Idling Type Supply System (Constant Volume)

Fig.3-2 shows an example of a non self idling supply system which is essentially the same as the self idling type with the exception of the following features.

(a) Engine Driven Pump
This type of pump provides a continuous flow of hydraulic fluid to the system and has no direct control over the system pressure. Note in Fig.3-2 there are only two pipes connected to this type of pump, the inlet from the reservoir and the outlet to the system. The pumping capacity of this type of pump for a given rpm is fixed, hence the terms constant volume or fixed volume pump. To control the system pressure this type of pump relies on an automatic cut out valve.

(b) Automatic Cut Out Valve
In simple terms the automatic cut out valve is a sensitive pressure relief valve which is fitted after the pump and when system pressure is reached the automatic cut out will close the pipeline to the system and return, or redirect, the fluid from the pump back to the reservoir. The detailed operation of this component will be discussed in the components chapter.

(c) Accumulator
Essentially the accumulator is used to store fluid under pressure and is fitted to hydraulic systems to serve a number of functions. Firstly, it is fitted adjacent to the automatic cut out valve to ensure it operates correctly by providing a back pressure on the cut out valve to prevent what is termed 'hydraulic hammering'. This is a condition which causes the cut out valve to open and close rapidly creating the hammering effect which in turn sends shock waves through the

hydraulic pipelines that will cause damage to the pipelines, components and seals within the system.

Secondly, the accumulator will also provide pressure to give initial impetus to components when they are selected. When a selection is made the operation of the pump may be too slow to react to an instant demand, the accumulator will make up for this loss.

Thirdly, the accumulator will compensate for any temporary drop in pressure within the system.

Fourthly, the accumulator will also provide fluid under pressure for emergency operation of certain services, such as wheel brakes.

Finally, the action of the engine driven pump tends to create a pulsating flow due to the nature of its principle of operation, the accumulator is used to smooth out minor pressure fluctuations of this nature.

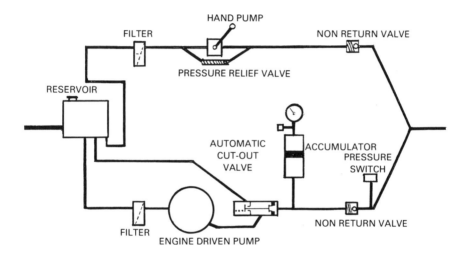

Fig.3-2. Non Self Idling Supply System (Constant Volume Pump).

Note: Ground Service Connections are not shown in this figure.

(d) General

Fig.3-2 shows the position of the pressure switch in a different location to that in Fig.3-1. This is for clarity purposes only.

3.5 Two Pump Supply System

Fig.3-3 shows an example of a two pump supply system. Some systems are fitted with a number of pumps to provide a number of essential requirements, the most important of which is safety. In the example shown in Fig.3-3 in the event one pump fails supply system fluid can still be maintained.

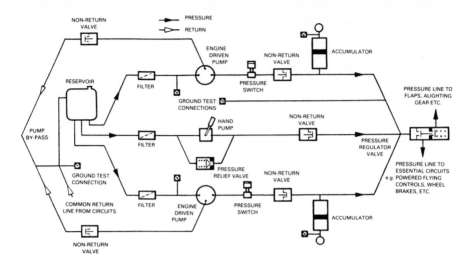

Fig.3-3. Two Pump Supply System.

The system shown in Fig.3-3 is fitted with two self idling (variable volume) pumps which, should one pump fail, will still provide fluid flow but at half normal rate. In such an event the operating times of services will be doubled, for example, an undercarriage that takes twelve seconds to retract will now take twenty four seconds to retract. System pressure will still remain constant.

It is sometimes difficult to understand what is meant by an Essential Service within the context of a hydraulic system, to answer this an explanation is given of each basic service and the operation of that service in an emergency.

Firstly, the system is divided into two specific groups which are termed:

Primary Services

and

Secondary Services

(a) Primary Services

These services are also commonly known as essential services and are services which, in the event of total failure, will result in the aircraft being unable to remain in controlled flight. An example of such a service are the Powered Flying Control Units, a form of hydraulic actuator which operates the primary flying controls such as elevators, ailerons and rudder.

Many aircraft have the ability to revert to manual operation in the event of hydraulic failure to maintain control of the aircraft in systems where powered flying controls are fitted. However, an increasing number of modern aircraft are very difficult to control in manual operation, or in some cases rely totally on hydraulic actuation without any manual reversion.

On such systems it is essential to provide back up hydraulic systems for obvious safety reasons, if, however, problems still persist, provision must be made to reserve what hydraulic pressure is remaining in the system for essential services.

To this end, the pressure maintaining valve is fitted so that when system pressure falls below a certain value it will close off supply of fluid to non-essential services. Note — that it is possible the pressure loss could be due to a leak in a non essential service. As can be seen in Fig.3-4 the fluid pressure that is remaining will only be directed to the powered flying control units.

(b) Secondary Services

Whilst these services are often termed non-essential services, this is only in the context of hydraulic fluid supply. For example the lowering of the undercarriage prior to landing is an essential function, however, in an emergency it can be lowered by employing other methods. The following is a list of methods employed to operate services in the event of total hydraulic supply failure.

(1) Undercarriage or Alighting Gear

These systems are often lowered in an emergency by the use of compressed air or nitrogen which is stored in the aircraft for such an event.

(2) Flaps

In a similar manner to the undercarriage the flaps may be lowered on landing by the use of compressed air or nitrogen.

(3) Wheel Brakes

Emergency brakes are provided with accumulators which store sufficient fluid under pressure for a complete landing run plus a reserve factor.

(4) Hydraulically Operated Doors

The majority of hydraulically operated doors and similar devices have override systems which allow them to be operated manually.

(5) Air or Speed Brakes

In an emergency such as total hydraulic failure these would only be used on landing and would be operated by compressed air or nitrogen.

3.6 Pressure Maintaining Valve

Whilst this component is not strictly part of the supply system it does have a direct influence over the supply of fluid to certain hydraulic circuits within the aircraft. To help understand its function Fig.3-4 shows the relationship between the supply system and the other circuits within the complete aircraft hydraulic system.

The detailed operation of such emergency services will be discussed later in this book.

Note: An alternative name given to the pressure maintaining valve by some manufacturers is the 'Pressure Regulator Valve'.

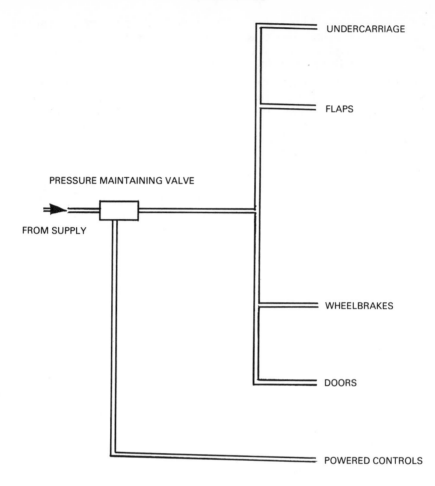

Fig.3-4. Aircraft Hydraulic System.

3.7 Priority Valve

In the past the name Priority Valve has been used to describe a component similar to the pressure maintaining valve, however, in modern hydraulic systems the priority valve is used in place of the pressure maintaining valve and is electrically operated. In the event a hydraulic leak occurs in a hydraulic system the fluid level in the reservoir will progressively fall. A fluid level switch is located within the reservoir which will be activated when the fluid level falls to a certain point, this in turn will send an electrical signal to the priority valve causing it to close off supply to non-essential services and reserve what fluid is left in the system for essential services only. This provides a much better arrangement than that provided by the pressure maintaining valve.

Fig.3-5 shows an example of its location within the system.

22

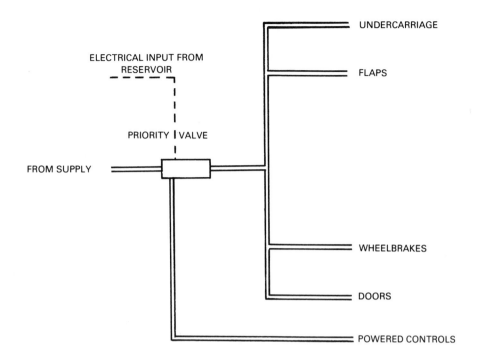

Fig.3-5. Priority Valve Location.

Note: On some aircraft the Priority Valve as shown above is also known as a Pressure Maintaining Valve. As can be seen they perform essentially the same function in protecting the Primary, or Essential services.

TEST YOURSELF 3
SUPPLY SYSTEMS

1. In a supply system using a variable volume pump, system pressure is controlled by:
   (a) the automatic cut out valve.
   (b) the accumulator.
   (c) the pressure regulator valve.
   (d) the pump itself.

   Ref. 3.4.

2. An accumulator:
   (a) is fitted prior to the automatic cut out valve.
   (b) gives initial impetus when a service is selected.
   (c) is only used in an emergency.
   (d) is fitted between the reservoir and the pump.

   Ref. 3.4.

3. When the variable volume pump is in the idle position:
   (a) no fluid is allowed to pass through the pump.
   (b) a small amount of fluid is allowed to pass through the pump.
   (c) the automatic cut out valve is open to return.
   (d) the pump is stopped.

   Ref. 3.3.

4. In order to provide a head of pressure, the reservoir:
   (a) is sometimes pressurised.
   (b) is provided with an accumulator.
   (c) is fitted below the level of the engine driven pump.
   (d) is fitted with a relief valve.

   Ref. 3.3.

5. Warning of pressure failure in a hydraulic supply system is provided by:
   (a) a supply system pressure gauge.
   (b) audible warning only.
   (c) a pressure warning light.
   (d) a mechanical indicator.

   Ref. 3.3.

6. In a supply system using a constant volume engine driven pump system pressure:
   (a) is controlled by the accumulator.
   (b) is controlled by the reservoir.
   (c) is controlled by the automatic cut out valve.
   (d) is controlled by the pressure switch.

   Ref. 3.4.

7. On modern large aircraft the hand pump:
   (a) provides fluid flow for ground servicing.
   (b) provides emergency pressure.
   (c) acts as a transfer pump between reservoirs.
   (d) is used to prime the engine driven pumps before starting.

   Ref. 3.3.

8. The low pressure filter of a hydraulic supply system is fitted:
   (a) between the reservoir and pump.
   (b) immediately after the pump.
   (c) within the pump assembly.
   (d) in the return line.

   Ref. 3.3.

9. The automatic cut out valve is assisted in its operation by:
   (a) the pressure switch.
   (b) the head of pressure provided by the reservoir.
   (c) the accumulator.
   (d) the hand pump.

   Ref. 3.4.

10. Variations in supply system volume due to ram displacement is compensated for by:
   (a) the accumulator.
   (b) the reservoir.
   (c) the automatic cut out valve.
   (d) the pressure switch.

   Ref. 3.3.

4

FLAP CIRCUIT

4.1 Introduction

Firstly, it is important to realise that the operation of the flaps must be of a slow and smooth nature avoiding any rapid or erratic trim changes to the aircraft. It must also be noted that unlike many systems, such as the undercarriage, the flaps require to be selected in a number of positions and not just in the fully up, or fully down positions, as a result provision must be made in the hydraulic system to cater for these requirements.

4.2 Selector or Control Valve

The flap system control valve is operated from the cockpit by the operation of a lever which may operate the system control valve electrically or by a system of mechanical push/pull rods and levers. The actual control valve has three basic positions, firstly a position which directs the fluid to the jack, or actuator, to move the flaps down, normally termed the down line. Also a selection to cause the flaps to move toward the up position, which in turn is normally called the up line.

It must be noted when flaps are selected down the pressure to move the flaps down is applied to the down line, at the same time the return fluid from the other side of the jack piston is returned via the line which would normally be called the up line, through the selector and back to the reservoir through the common return line.

The third control valve position is a neutral position which creates what is termed a hydraulic lock, which when in this position will not allow fluid into or out of the flap circuit. When flaps are selected to maximum lift position for example, the flaps will move down to that position with fluid under pressure directed through the flap down line. On arrival at the maximum lift position the control valve will move to the neutral position thereby preventing any further movement of the flaps until a further selection is made. The details of the control valves are given later in the chapter on components.

4.3 Non-Return Valve

A non-return valve is usually fitted just prior to the control valve, or is incorporated within the control valve assembly, and prevents interference between services. Such interference takes the form of the operation of one service drawing fluid from the other usually due to cavitation problems. For example without a non-return valve fitted in this position, and with flaps fully down, when the alighting gear is selected down, it would be possible for the undercarriage jacks to draw fluid from the flap circuit causing the flaps to return to an up position.

4.4 Two Way Restrictor

In order to achieve a smooth slow operation of the flaps a two way restrictor valve is fitted in the down line of the flap circuit. By positioning the valve in this way the movement rate of the flaps will be controlled in both the up and down selections.

Note: The two way restrictor may be replaced in some systems by a THROTTLING VALVE, or a FLOW CONTROL VALVE.

On larger aircraft a more complex type of fluid flow control is required, these valves will be discussed later.

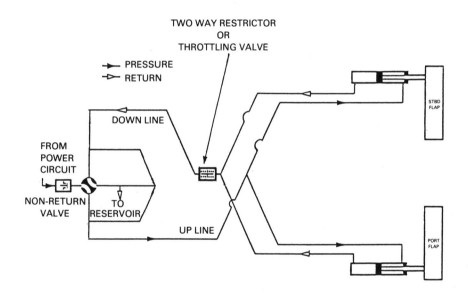

Fig.4-1. Flap Circuit.

4.5 Pressure Relief Valve

As has been previously stated, flaps are sometimes required to be selected to a position between fully up and fully down, such as the maximum lift position. When this selection is made from flaps fully up the fluid will flow through the down line, its flow restricted by the two way restrictor, moving the flap jacks to the maximum lift position. When that position is reached, the selector is moved to a neutral position, which will stop fluid flow into or out of the flap circuit, creating a hydraulic lock. Under these conditions system pressure is held within the flap circuit to prevent the flaps moving due to the forces of the airflow acting on them. In this condition of operation, should the fluid trapped in the flap circuit be subjected to increased temperatures, the hydraulic fluid will expand, usually termed thermal expansion. Such expansion may create forces strong enough to cause damage to the circuit, to such items as seals, pipe connections and to the components themselves. To prevent such damage, protection is provided within the circuit by pressure relief valves, normally having one fitted in the down line, the other in the up line.

Under normal operating conditions the fluid pressure would rise to a maximum of, for example, 3000 psi, the pressure relief valve may be set to open at 3050 psi so that in the event thermal expansion takes place due to excessive temperatures, when the pressure rises to 3050 psi the pressure relief valve will open returning some fluid back to the reservoir reducing the pressure in the flap circuit to within safe limits. As an example the pressure relief valve would close again at 2095 psi.

As will be explained in the component chapter there are various types of pressure relief valve, the type most commonly used for this specific purpose is normally called a Thermal Relief Valve. It is important to point out such valves are sensitive to pressure and not temperature.

Fig.4-2 shows the system in a situation of relieving excess pressure due to thermal expansion.

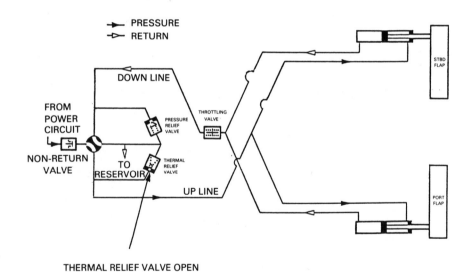

THERMAL RELIEF VALVE OPEN

Fig.4-2. Relief of Pressure Due to Thermal Expansion.

4.6 Flap Selection at Excessive Airspeed

As explained in the previous paragraph, let us assume that flaps are selected to the maximum lift position. If such a position of flap is selected at too high an airspeed, on most aircraft, damage to the flaps and their operating systems may result. To prevent this, two basic types of protection system are used; firstly, a system linked to the airspeed and the flap selector, whereby selection of the flaps above a given airspeed is prevented. The second type of system involves the hydraulic flap circuit.

If the flaps are selected down at excessive airspeeds the air loads on the flaps will be very high and in effect will try to push the flaps back to the fully up position. The loads on the flap surfaces created by the airflow will be transmitted through the flap operating mechanism and cause the hydraulic pressure in the flap circuit to rise. Under such circumstances the excessive pressure in the flap circuit will be relieved by the pressure relief valve in the down line which in turn will allow the flaps to be 'blown' back to the fully up position. In such a system the pressure relief valve is known as the 'Blow Back Valve' and must be capable of relieving a full flow rate of fluid.

Fig.4-3 shows an example of a flap circuit fitted with a blow back valve.

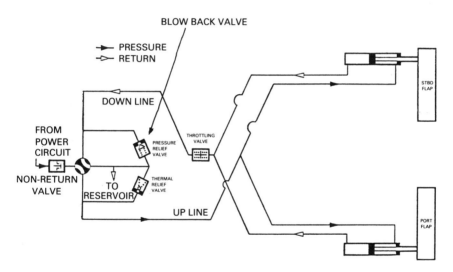

Fig.4-3. Flap Circuit with a Blow Back Valve.

4.7 Flap Jacks (Actuators)

The purpose of the flap jack is to convert the hydraulic pressure generated by the hydraulic supply system into mechanical energy. As has been previously stated, the flaps must move smoothly in both directions to avoid rapid trim changes of the aircraft and in order that this is achieved the flaps are normally equipped with balanced, or equal area piston jacks. An example is shown in Fig.4-4.

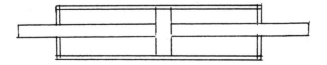

Fig.4-4. Equal Area Piston Jack.

It must be noted however, not all flaps are operated by balanced piston jacks.

4.8 Synchronisation of Flaps

It is vital that when flaps are selected that both port and starboard flaps move together in a synchronised manner and in order to achieve this one of a number of methods may be used.

(a) Single Jack Method

This method uses one jack or actuator to move both flaps. The flaps are interconnected by mechanical means ensuring that both port and starboard flaps must move together at all times. The major disadvantage of this method is that the link mechanism between port and starboard flap assemblies must pass through the fuselage from one wing to the other. On some aircraft this may not be acceptable because of the valuable space taken up by the jack and operating mechanism and so an alternative method must be used.

(b) Flap Synchronising Circuit

Many flap systems use the principle of a flap synchronising circuit to balance the pressure and flow rates to the flaps to ensure the flaps move together.

Fig.4-5 shows an example of such a system.

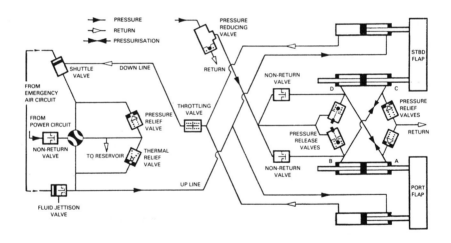

Fig.4-5. Flap Synchronising Circuit included in Flap Circuit.

Operation

Due to variations in jack volume, or piston friction, or to unequal air loads on the flaps during landing, the rate at which the port and starboard flaps move may differ. To avoid, or minimise this possibility the flaps are normally synchronised. There are many ways in which this may be achieved and this example is included in order to give you a basic idea of one such system.

30

The system shown in Fig.4-5 employs the use of two additional jacks which are of an equal area type and are positioned inboard of the main jacks. There are also two pressure release valves, two non-return valves, two pressure relief valves, and a pressure reducing valve.

Normal supply pressure is in the order of 3000 psi and the pressure reducing valve reduces the pressure to the synchronising circuit to 500 psi and ensure the circuit is not over-pressurised. The pressure relief valves will open to relieve excess pressure should the pressure reducing valve fail in any way, or if the flaps are subjected to excessive external force causing the hydraulic pressure to rise above 500 psi.

The non-return valves isolate the sychronising circuit ensuring the transfer fluid moves direct from jack to jack. The fluid in the synchronising jacks is merely transferred when the flaps travel in alignment, but should there be a tendency for the rate of travel of one flap to be slower than the other flap, then the synchronising jack on the slow flap will provide an assisting force to the slow operating jack.

For example, assume that flaps DOWN has been selected and that the port flap tends to move down faster than the starboard flap. The piston in the port synchronising jack would expel more fluid from A to D than D can temporarily accommodate, therefore pressure is generated in D which, acting on the piston of the starboard synchronising jack, produces an assisting force helping to keep the starboard flap in alignment with the port flap. The fluid expelled from C is accommodated in B.

If there is a slight variation in synchronising jack capacities, they would move increasingly out of phase with each other. To prevent this pressure release valves are fitted which open mechanically, by a plunger being depressed every time the flaps move to the fully up position. The depression of the plungers open the fluid way up between the two synchronising jacks. At this time any loss of fluid due to small leakages is also compensated for by the supply via the pressure reducing valve.

TEST YOURSELF 4
FLAP CIRCUIT

1. To prevent rapid trim changes of the aircraft when flaps are selected down:
   (a) the flap selector is fitted with a neutral position.
   (b) balanced piston jacks are fitted.
   (c) a one way restrictor is fitted.
   (d) a two way restrictor may be fitted.

   Ref. 4.4.

2. In the event flaps may be selected at too high an airspeed, a:
   (a) two way restrictor is fitted in the down line.
   (b) two way restrictor is fitted in the up line.
   (c) thermal relief valve is fitted in the down line.
   (d) pressure relief valve is fitted in the down line.

   Ref. 4.6.

3. A 'Blow Back' valve is:
   (a) a thermal relief valve.
   (b) a pressure relief valve.
   (c) a two way restrictor.
   (d) a sequence valve.

   Ref. 4.6.

4. When flaps are selected at maximum lift:
   (a) a hydraulic lock is created.
   (b) the flap circuit becomes an open circuit.
   (c) the selector creates an open circuit.
   (d) the blow back valve is open.

   Ref. 4.2.

5. Excessive pressure in a flap circuit due to thermal expansion:
   (a) is relieved by a thermal relief valve.
   (b) is allowed back to return via the selector.
   (c) is not a problem.
   (d) is relieved by the two way restrictor.

   Ref. 4.5.

5

UNDERCARRIAGE CIRCUIT

5.1 Introduction

The undercarriage circuit illustrated in Fig.5-1 consists of two main undercarriage jacks and a nose undercarriage jack. There is also a door jack for each of the undercarriage unit doors. In order to appreciate the operation of hydraulic system a basic understanding of the undercarriage sequence is essential. The system in question provides the following:

On take off undercarriage UP is selected and each of the undercarriage legs are retracted, when they reach the fully up position the undercarriage doors close.

On DOWN selection, the doors open fully before the undercarriage legs extend.

On some aircraft the doors close again when the undercarriage legs reach the fully down position: not shown in the illustrated system. For clarity only one undercarriage leg is illustrated in Fig.5-1.

5.2 Operation (UP Selection)

When undercarriage up is selected, fluid enters the undercarriage circuit via the control valve and is directed to the UP line. UP line in this context means the pipeline through which the fluid flows to move the undercarriage to the UP position. The fluid flows firstly through a One-Way Restrictor, which in this selection allows full unrestricted flow through the valve. After flowing through the one-way restrictor the fluid flows to the undercarriage leg jack; take note it cannot flow through the mechanical sequence valve to the door jack until the plunger of the mechanical sequence valve is depressed and the valve opened. The mechanical sequence valve will be opened by the final UP movement of the undercarriage jack as it almost reaches the fully up position. Once the mechanical sequence valve is opened the fluid can now flow to the door jack and close the undercarriage door.

The return fluid has a free passage back to return via the control valve.

5.3 Operation (DOWN Selection)

When the undercarriage is selected DOWN, fluid is directed firstly to the door jack which on operation opens the undercarriage door. The final movement of the door jack opens the mechanical sequence valve which in turn allows the fluid to flow to the undercarriage jack forcing the undercarriage down. The important element in the undercarriage DOWN selection to make particular note of is what happens to the return fluid. The return fluid is caused to flow through a one-way restrictor valve in the restricted direction, this action has the effect of slowing down the undercarriage operation as it is lowering, or extending. This action is essential to prevent cavitation in the under-carriage down line.

Undercarriages when selected have tendency to' free-fall due mainly to their weight.

Once selected and with the up lock disengaged, the pump flow rate would not normally be able to combat the suction effect caused by the undercarriage falling. This effect can be minimised by the fitting of a one-way restrictor. See Fig.5-1.

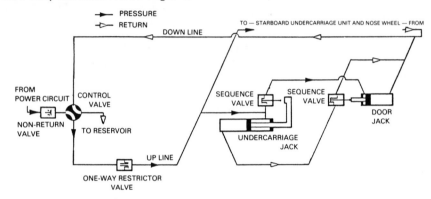

Fig.5-1. Position of One-Way Restrictor.

Note: This problem does not arise when an UP selection is made.

Thermal Relief Valves
The undercarriage circuit is effectively a closed circuit on many aircraft when the undercarriage is in the fully UP or fully DOWN positions. Due to this any significant increase in temperature may result in expansion of the fluid causing an excessive pressure increase. This increase of pressure is relieved through thermal valves which are located one in the UP line and one in the DOWN line. See Fig.5-2.

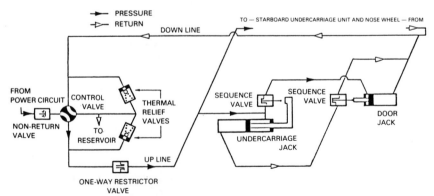

Fig.5-2. Location of Thermal Relief Valves.

5.4 Pressure Regulator Valve (Special)

Some undercarriage systems are fitted with this valve unit to eliminate certain additional problems that may arise.

When undercarriage UP is selected, the undercarriage moves to the fully retracted position and the door closes. Problems may arise, however, when the undercarriage has retracted and the door is closing, for there may be a tendency for the pressure to fall in the undercarriage jack, which will cause the undercarriage to 'droop'. This may further result in the undercarriage door colliding with the undercarriage. This valve ensures that sufficient pressure is maintained in the undercarriage jack to keep the undercarriage retracted whilst the door is closing. See Fig.5-3.

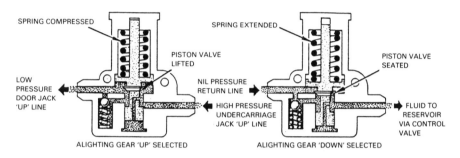

Fig.5-3. Operation of Pressure Regulator Valve (Special)

5.5 Sequence Valve Hydraulic

When the undercarriage is selected DOWN, the doors open and the undercarriage is lowered. To prevent the fall in pressure between door jack and undercarriage jack from causing the door to partially close when the undercarriage jack is extending, a sequence valve hydraulic is fitted to the UP line. This valve, which is hydraulically operated by fluid pressure in the Down line, ensures that adequate pressure is maintained in the door jack to keep the door open while the undercarriage is being lowered. See Fig.5-4.

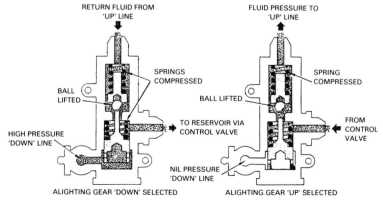

Fig.5-4. Sequence Valve Hydraulic.

5.6 Mechanical Sequence Valve

When fluid pressure is present at connection (1) the valve assembly is seated and the fluid flow is stopped until the plunger is depressed. With the reversal of the flow, the fluid pressure at connection (2) will overcome the pressure of the spring, lift the valve assembly and fluid will flow to connection (1). Since the fluid connections are not directly opposed, one feeds the back of the valve assembly and the other feeds the valve face. When fluid is trapped behind the valve, the fluid pressure assists in maintaining the valve on its seat.

The plunger is operated by the final action of the door or the undercarriage in its movements.

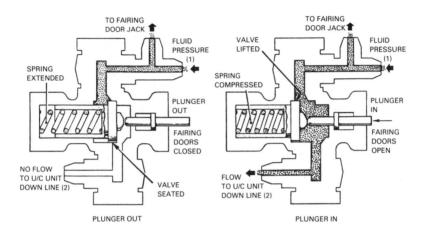

Fig.5-5. Mechanical Sequence Valve.

TEST YOURSELF 5
UNDERCARRIAGES

1. The sequence of operation of the undercarriage legs and doors is controlled by:
   (a) the mechanical sequence valves.
   (b) the sequence valve hydraulic.
   (c) the pressure regulator valve.
   (d) the pressure regulator valve special.

Ref. 5.2.

2. Cavitation in the undercarriage circuit when the undercarriage is selected up:
   (a) is prevented by the two way restrictor.
   (b) is prevented by the one way restrictor.
   (c) is prevented by the mechanical sequence valves.
   (d) is not a problem.

Ref. 5.2.

3. The pressure regulator valve special prevents:
   (a) the door drooping as the undercarriage is retracting.
   (b) the undercarriage drooping as the undercarriage retracts.
   (c) the undercarriage drooping as the door closes.
   (d) the door closing as the undercarriage extends.

Ref. 5.4.

4. Cavitation when undercarriage DOWN is selected is prevented by:
   (a) the mechanical sequence valves.
   (b) the two way restrictor.
   (c) the regulator valve.
   (d) the one way restrictor.

Ref. 5.3.

5. The mechanical sequence valves are operated:
   (a) from the cockpit.
   (b) by the final movement of the undercarriage or door.
   (c) by the undercarriage doors only.
   (d) by the undercarriages only.

Ref. 5.2 and 3.

6

WHEEL BRAKE CIRCUIT

6.1 Introduction

The wheel brakes of a modern aircraft provide a number of functions, the most vital of which is braking the aircraft on its landing run. On many light and medium sized aircraft the wheel brakes also provide the means of steering the aircraft on the ground, during the landing run and also when taxying. Through all these functions the wheel brakes must provide a capability of progressive braking, differential braking, and also some form of emergency braking.

Progressive Braking is:
The ability of the system to progressively increase brake pressure.

Differential Braking is:
The ability of the system to be used to steer the aircraft on the ground.

6.2 Wheel Brake System

Fig.6-1 shows an example of an aircraft wheel brake system.

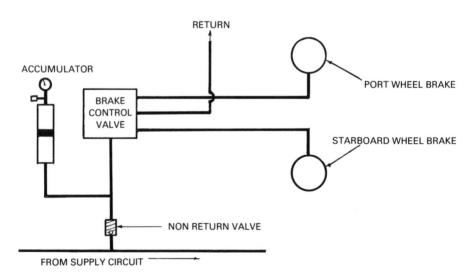

Fig.6-1.

Under normal operating conditions the wheel brake circuit is supplied with fluid under pressure by the hydraulic supply system. The fluid on entering the circuit passes through a non-return valve, this prevents fluid from flowing back out of the system, particularly in the event of main system failure. Between the non-return valve and brake control valve is situated the brake accumulator.

6.3   Wheel Brake Hydraulic Accumulator

When brakes are not in use the accumulator is charged by the supply system with fluid to maximum normal working pressure. When brakes are applied they are required to provide instant response and a delay while the supply system builds up pressure would not be acceptable. In this instance, the accumulator gives initial impetus to the brake units allowing them to operate instantly. The accumulator will again be recharged with fluid under pressure when the brakes are not being used. The accumulator will also damp out fluctuations in pressure to provide smooth braking, an essential requirement on the landing run, and provides a store of fluid pressure available for brake applications in the event the supply system should fail.

6.4   Brake Control Valve

When a selection is made the brake control valve directs fluid under pressure to the wheel brake units. Firstly it performs the function of a pressure reducing valve in that it reduces system pressure to a lower value. This is usually the case with brakes in that they operate at a lower pressure than most other hydraulic services.

When either pilot's brake pedals are depressed on the appropriate side of the cockpit, or the hand operated brake lever is applied, the servo valve applies load to the linkage on the control valve, which via the lever assembly and plunger, presses down the exhaust cap. This action initially closes the gap between the exhaust valve cap and the exhaust

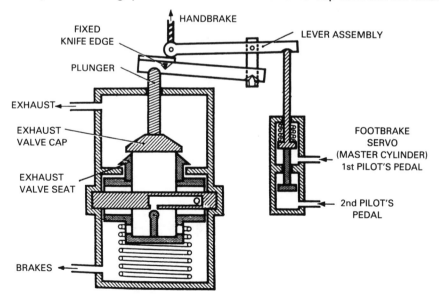

Fig.6-2. Brake Control Valve Mechanism.

valve seat, then moves the cradle down to open the inlet valve, and direct the fluid to the brakes. Pressure builds up in the brakes and valve until it is sufficient, assisted by the spring, to overcome the inlet pressure, to force the cradle and exhaust valve seat against the exhaust valve cap, and to close the inlet valve. An increase in the load applied to the valve linkage will be balanced by the increased delivery pressure, and a decrease in the load applied will be balanced by the relief of delivery pressure past the exhaust valve. When the brake pedals are released, the exhaust valve cap lifts and exhausts pressure from the brakes to the reservoir.

A handbrake lever is provided in order that the brakes may be applied when the aircraft is stationary on the ground.

Fig.6-2 shows the brake control valve operating mechanism.

6.5   Anti-Skid Units

Fig.6-3 shows a brake system with Anti-Skid Units fitted. A detailed description of anti-skid units is given in the volume on undercarriages in this series, only a basic description of the purpose of an anti-skid unit is given here.

When brakes are applied and pressure is progressively increased there may be a tendency for the wheel to lock, that is skid. At this point the anti-skid unit releases some pressure from the brake unit to avoid the wheel being locked, this fluid is then directed back to the common return line from the anti-skid unit. In effect the anti-skid unit allows the brakes to be applied and released at a very rapid rate repeatedly avoiding the wheels skidding. This tends to create shock waves in the hydraulic fluid which may damage the system and so to prevent such shock waves a Modulator Valve is fitted to smooth out brake operation.

The Anti-Skid System allows the brake to be applied at maximum pressure from the point of touch down and so produces a much shorter landing run.

6.6   Fig.6-4 Shows an Example of a Modulator Valve

A Modulator Valve is fitted in the brake circuit in conjunction with the anti-skid unit to reduce the shock waves discussed in paragraph 6.5. The valve allows full flow of fluid to the brake unit on initial brake application and thereafter restricts the flow. During initial operation of the brakes, the piston is forced down the cylinder against spring

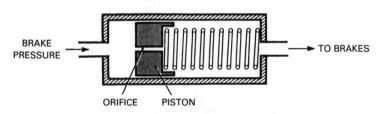

Fig.6-4. Modulator Valve.

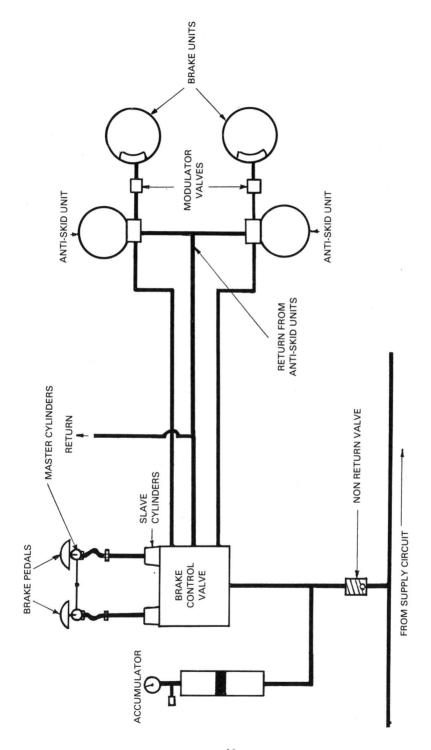

Fig.6-3. Brake System with Anti-Skid Units.

pressure, and the brakes are applied. Subsequent fluid feed to the brakes, necessitated by the anti-skid unit operation, is through the restricted orifice, and is very limited. This limited flow allows the anti-skid unit to completely release the brakes when required, i.e. when approaching a skid, and conserves main system pressure. When the control valve is released, the piston returns to its original position under the influence of the spring and return fluid.

TEST YOURSELF 6
WHEEL BRAKE CIRCUIT

1. The wheel brake accumulator provides:
   (a) emergency braking only.
   (b) initial impetus when brakes are applied.
   (c) emergency pressure for all circuits.
   (d) no emergency pressure.
   Ref. 6.3.

2. The N.R.V. in a brake circuit is fitted:
   (a) after the accumulator.
   (b) after the brake control valve.
   (c) between the supply and the accumulator.
   (d) between the control valve and the brake unit.
   Ref. 6.2.

3. A Modulator Valve is fitted in a brake circuit to:
   (a) assist in operation when an anti-skid unit is fitted.
   (b) prevent loss of pressure when wheelbrakes lock.
   (c) prevent loss of fluid when supply pressure fails.
   (d) prevent loss of pressure when the control valve fails.
   Ref. 6.6.

4. A Modulator Valve is fitted:
   (a) between the control valve and the accumulator.
   (b) between the control valve and the anti-skid unit.
   (c) between the anti-skid unit and the brake.
   (d) between the N.R.V. and the control valve.
   Ref. 6.6.

5. Differential Braking is:
   (a) a progressive increase of brake pressure.
   (b) a system having more than one brake unit per wheel.
   (c) a system where the brakes are used to steer the aircraft.
   (d) a system where the brakes are duplicated.
   Ref. 6.1.

7

NOSE WHEEL STEERING

7.1 Introduction

Modern aircraft are steered on the ground by one of two methods. Most light and medium sized aircraft are steered on the ground by differential braking. This method employs the principle of applying brake hydraulic pressure to the wheel brake on either the port or starboard side of the aircraft to achieve directional control by retarding the wheel on the selected side. In this type of system the nose, or tailwheel, is allowed to freely castor.

On large aircraft, particularly those with multi-wheel main undercarriage units, the ability to control the aircraft through a nose wheel steering mechanism is desirable. In most cases nose wheel steering is achieved through a hydraulically operated mechanism.

7.2 Requirements of the System

There are several basic requirements that must be catered for in the design of a nose wheel steering system.

(a) Castoring

When an aircraft is being moved on the ground, employing a towing vehicle, the nosewheel assembly must be free to castor, that is rotate about a vertical axis, in order that directional control through the towing vehicle and towing arm can be achieved. This point must be noted when studying the system.

(b) Shimmy

Some means must be provided to dampen shimmy when landing. Shimmy is, or can become, violent castoring of the nose wheel from side to side usually initiated by cross winds or uneven surfaces and can lead to serious vibration resulting in damage or loss of directional control. Shimmy may be minimised by dampers.

(c) Control

The nose wheel steering system is normally controlled by a small steering wheel situated in the cockpit and is instinctive in much the same way as a car steering wheel.

(d) Self Centring

In all nose wheel steering systems it is essential to provide a self-centring system to ensure the nose wheel is in line with the nose wheel undercarriage bay when the undercarriage is retracted on take off. Failure to return to the centre position may result in serious damage to the undercarriage and the aircraft structure.

7.3 Operation

Essentially a nose wheel steering system is a servo system in much the same way as Powered Flying Controls.

As the steering wheel is moved, the operating cables cause the slide selector (1) to move against the action of a self-centring spring. When in the centre position the selector permits the nose wheel to castor freely. In this situation if the aircraft is being towed on the ground the nose wheel may freely castor with the fluid being transferred through the selector from one jack to the other when powered steering is not required. The steering is affected by a pair of jacks (2) fed from the selector through a pair of restrictor valves. The restrictor valves (3) are of the two-way type and act as shimmy dampers when steering is not in use such as on the landing run. A double relief valve (4) prevents excessive pressure being set up in the jacks if the nose wheel castors violently. To maintain oil in the steering jacks at all times, a low pressure relief valve with a spring loaded piston (5) is used in the return line from the selector. When the pilot wants to steer he pulls the wheel towards him, thus closing a switch which energises the selector (6) and applies pressure to the system. A hydraulic pressure reducing valve (7) may be used to reduce the pressure in the jacks. A three-way selector (6) is used in place of a simple on/off selector in order to offload the selector when self-centring is required.

See Fig.7-1.

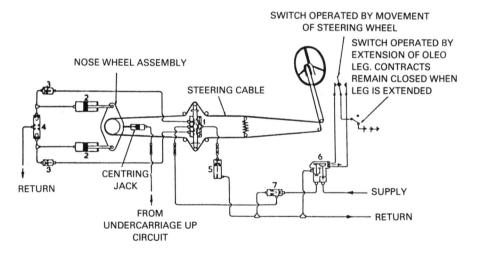

Fig.7-1. Nose-wheel Steering Circuit.

7.4 Single Jack Systems

Many of the modern nose wheel steering systems use a single jack which is of the balanced piston type. This saves weight, space and cost and is just as effective.

TEST YOURSELF 7
NOSE WHEEL STEERING

1. Shimmy is:
   - (a) the ability of the nose wheel to freely castor.
   - (b) damped by two pressure relief valves.
   - (c) damped by two restrictor valves.
   - (d) damped by the self-centring jacks.

   Ref. 7.2.

2. Excessive pressure is prevented from building up in the jacks due to violent castoring by:
   - (a) two restrictor valves.
   - (b) a double acting pressure relief valve.
   - (c) a two-way restrictor.
   - (d) the selector.

   Ref. 7.3.

3. The Self-Centring Jack:
   - (a) centres the nose wheel prior to retraction.
   - (b) centres the nose wheel prior to extension.
   - (c) centres the nose wheel during steering.
   - (d) centres the nose wheel in an emergency.

   Ref. 7.2.

4. Control of nose wheel steering on modern aircraft is effected through:
   - (a) a steering wheel.
   - (b) rudder pedals.
   - (c) a steering bar.
   - (d) a steering lever.

   Ref. 7.1.

5. Shimmy may be caused by:
   - (a) excessive oil pressure.
   - (b) over-inflated tyres.
   - (c) a side wind on landing.
   - (d) a faulty selector.

   Ref. 7.2.

8

POWERED
FLYING CONTROLS

8.1 Introduction

Modern aircraft which fly at high speeds experience very high loads on their control surfaces. Such loads are beyond the help or assistance which may be provided by fitting spring tabs, servo tabs or balance tabs. An alternative and more effective form of assistance to the pilot is with the use of Power Operated Controls or Power Assisted Controls which are hydraulically actuated. The Power Operated and Power Assisted actuator units may be identical, the only major difference is the way in which they are installed. The following therefore is a description of a basic unit and its operation. Its installation will be discussed later.

8.2 Power Operated Control Unit — General

The Powered Flying Control Unit (PFCU), or actuator, is normally supplied by two independent hydraulic supply systems so that in the event one system fails, control of the aircraft is not lost. Some types of aircraft have also been fitted with manual reversion, that is the ability to revert back to manual operation in the event of hydraulic failure. The hydraulic system normally supplies the PFCUs via a Pressure Maintaining Valve or a Priority Valve so that in the event of a hydraulic fault resulting in a reduced system pressure, or a reduction in fluid content in the reservoir, the PFCUs are protected by isolation of all secondary services. The PFCUs are considered to be an Essential or Primary Service.

8.3 Powered Flying Control Unit Operation

The PFCU normally consists of two essential elements in the form of an actuator, or jack, to which is attached a selector valve.

Fluid under pressure is connected to the selector valve inlet. The selector, or Servo Valve is selected by the pilot when movements of the control column or rudder pedals are made. Fig.8-1 illustrates a simple example of a PFCU. Movement of the cockpit control moves the Servo Valve input via cables or rods, which determines the direction of fluid flow to one side or the other of the piston. The fluid cannot move the piston as the piston rod, or ram, is connected to the aircraft structure and the result is that the unit body moves and through linkage moves the control surface.

This action creates a follow up motion so that when a small input is made the body will move until the ports close. In this way the movement of the unit is always related to the movement of the cockpit control. Each time an input is made to the servo valve the body will move until the ports are closed when the servo valve is in neutral. Return fluid is also controlled and directed by the servo valve and when allowed to flow is directed back to the common return. When the servo valve is in neutral a hydraulic lock is formed so that the control surface is held rigidly in the selected position.

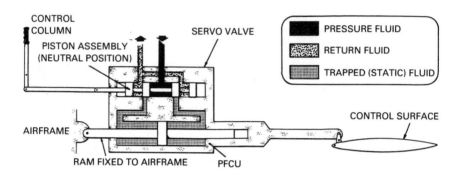

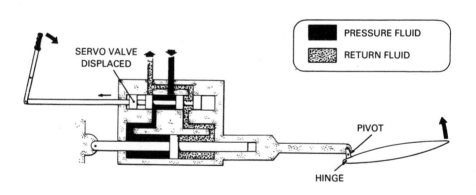

Fig.8-1. Simple PFCU.

8.4 Power Assisted and Powered Control

In a Power Assisted System the pilot is assisted in the operation of the control surface in the real sense in that the majority of the work of moving the control surface is done by the actuator and a small proportion is done by the pilot. This is shown by the examples illustrated in Fig.8-2 A and B showing a comparison of installations of Power Assisted and Powered Control. In the Powered Control System the actuator does all the work and the pilot's contribution of effort to move the control surface is zero.

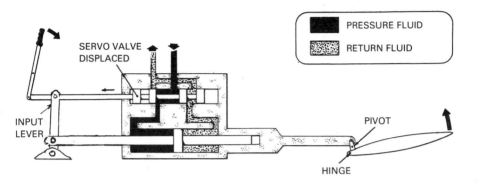

Fig.8-2A. Power Assisted System.

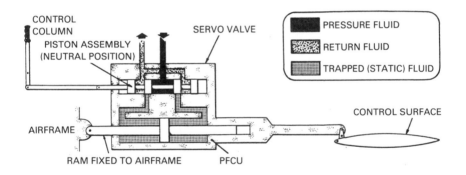

Fig.8-2B. Power Operated System.

8.5 Feel

On a Power Assisted installation the pilot feels a proportion of the load on the control surfaces and therefore can be said to have 'feel' or a 'sense of feel'. This is achieved by proportional feedback in that most of the load acting on the control surface is transmitted via the actuator body, fluid, piston and piston ram back into the airframe through the attachment point, however a small proportion of the load will be transmitted back through the input lever and control run to the cockpit control which will be felt by the pilot.

At high speeds if the control surface is progressively deflected, the load on the control surface will progressively increase and so the feel experienced by the pilot will also progressively increase.

On a Power Operated, or fully Powered Unit no feedback to the pilot will occur, the effect of load on the control surface will be totally absorbed in the airframe. In such a case artificial feel will have to be provided for the pilot.

Feel Units are discussed in detail in the volume concerning advanced control systems.

8.6　Self Contained PFCUs

On many large aircraft the Powered Flying Control Unit is a self-contained unit which has its own built-in hydraulic system and does not rely on any external hydraulic supply.

Self contained PFCUs normally have a mechanical input from the pilot's control and an electrical supply.

TEST YOURSELF 8
POWERED FLYING CONTROLS

1. On a Powered Assisted Control System the pilot:
   - (a) has no sense of feel of the load on the control surface.
   - (b) feels the full load on the control surface.
   - (c) feels a proportion of the load that is on the control surface.
   - (d) does not require to feel the load on the control surface.

   Ref. 8.5.

2. Feel units are required when:
   - (a) servo tabs are fitted to aircraft.
   - (b) power assisted controls are fitted to aircraft.
   - (c) spring tabs are fitted to aircraft.
   - (d) power controls are fitted to aircraft.

   Ref. 8.5.

3. Powered Control Systems are:
   - (a) considered to be essential services.
   - (b) secondary services.
   - (c) non-essential services.
   - (d) always self-contained units.

   Ref. 8.3.

4. Movement of the control column, operates the PFCU:
   - (a) servo valve.
   - (b) actuator.
   - (c) release valve.
   - (d) follow up lever.

   Ref. 8.3.

5. In a Power Assisted Installation, the:
   - (a) PFCU casing is connected to the aircraft structure.
   - (b) PFCU ram is connected to the aircraft structure.
   - (c) PFCU ram is connected to the input lever.
   - (d) PFCU ram is connected to the control surface.

   Ref. 8.4.

9

HYDRAULIC COMPONENTS

9.1 Reservoir

The design of reservoirs vary considerably, however, they all perform the same basic functions.

(a) To provide a reserve of fluid to compensate for minor leakages in the system.

(b) To allow for jack ram displacement, i.e. the variations in fluid volume being returned depending on whether the jack is extended or retracted.

(c) To allow for expansion of fluid due to increase of temperature.

(d) To provide a space for returning fluid.

(e) To provide a head of pressure to prevent cavitation at the Engine Driven Pump.

(f) In some cases to provide a reserve of fluid for emergency purposes.

General Construction

The reservoir usually consists of a basic tank with a filler assembly at the top.

Within the filler neck is usually fitted a filter assembly to filter out foreign objects which may enter the reservoir when filling operations are carried out. The cap to the filler may, on some types, also incorporate a dipstick to enable the fluid level to be checked. Other types of reservoirs may incorporate a sight glass or a float and indicator to show the fluid level.

On many reservoir types the supply, or suction pipe, to the main engine driven pump consists of a flexible hose within the reservoir which is weighted at the end. This ensures, no matter what the attitude of the aircraft, that the end of the suction pipe is always in the fluid to ensure a good supply is maintained. Other types of reservoir may incorporate a stack, or stand pipe in the base of the reservoir to which the main supply to the engine driven pump is connected at its lower end. This is fitted to ensure that in the event an emergency hand pump is available, should there be a serious leak, or engine driven pump failure, some fluid will be retained for use by the hand pump in the base of the reservoir.

An important function of the reservoir is to ensure a good positive supply is maintained to the engine driven pump, failure to do so may result in cavitation, that is, the action of the suction of the engine driven pump may cause a depression or a semi-vacuum in the pipeline between the reservoir and the pump. This can be avoided by establishing a head of pressure which is normally achieved by one of two methods or a combination of both. The first is to position the reservoir well above the level of the pump, thus creating a head of pressure.

The other is to pressurise the reservoir. Older type reservoirs are often pressurised by air to 30–40 psi in the air space above the level of the fluid. The air pressure may be supplied by reduced pressure from engine air beed, or occasionally by controlled ram air. Some aircraft have in the past been equipped with a reservoir air storage cylinder which provides the air pressure.

More recent types of reservoir are pressurised by a jack system which is pressurised with system fluid pressure, with this system the air space above the fluid is also eliminated so reducing the possibility of air contaminating the system. This last type is known as a 'Bootstrap' reservoir.

The various types of reservoir are shown in Fig.9-1.

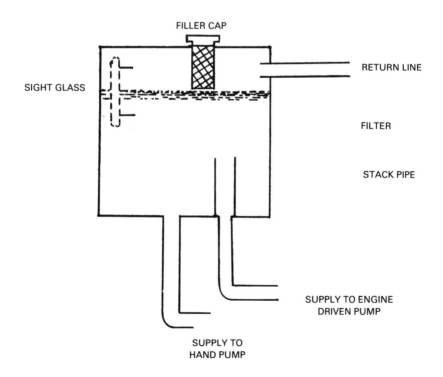

Fig.9-1. Hydraulic Reservoir with Stack Pipe.

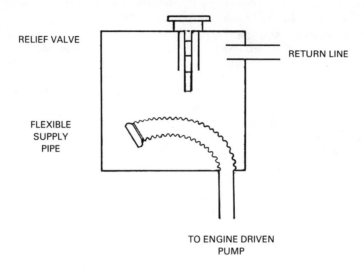

FILLER CAP WITH DIPSTICK

RELIEF VALVE

RETURN LINE

FLEXIBLE
SUPPLY
PIPE

TO ENGINE DRIVEN
PUMP

Fig.9-1B. Hydraulic Reservoir with Flexible Supply Pipe.

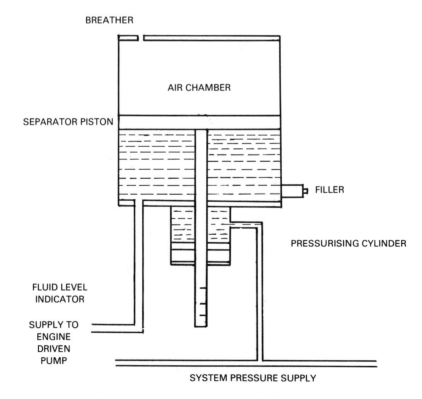

BREATHER

AIR CHAMBER

SEPARATOR PISTON

FILLER

PRESSURISING CYLINDER

FLUID LEVEL
INDICATOR

SUPPLY TO
ENGINE
DRIVEN
PUMP

SYSTEM PRESSURE SUPPLY

Fig-9.1C. Pressurised 'Bootstrap' Reservoir.

9.2 Filters

Filters tend to be divided into two distinct groups:

    (a)   Low Pressure or Suction Filters.

    (b)   High Pressure Filters.

(a) Low Pressure Filter

This type is often referred to as a suction filter which is the type most commonly fitted between the reservoir and the pump, both hand pump and engine driven pumps. They are often of simple design and normally minimise resistance to fluid flow. This is essential when fitted between the reservoir and pump in order to minimise cavitation at the pump.

An example of this filter is shown in Fig.9-2.

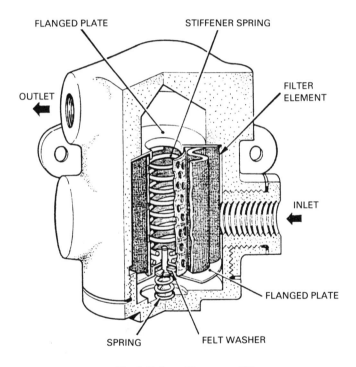

FLANGED PLATE   STIFFENER SPRING

OUTLET

FILTER
ELEMENT

INLET

FLANGED PLATE

SPRING   FELT WASHER

Fig.9-2. Low Pressure Filter.

(b) High Pressure Filter

The High Pressure Filter, sometimes termed a Pressure Filter, requires the system fluid to be under pressure in order to force it through the filter element and thereby remove any foreign matter from the fluid. Because of this, such filters will normally be fitted after the pump, i.e. on the pressure side of the pump, or downstream of the pump. In some cases high pressure filters may be fitted immediately after the pump or at the end of the supply system. Additional high pressure filters may also be fitted to individual circuits where the slightest contamination of the fluid may lead to serious damage or failure. Such a system, or circuit, is the Powered Flying Control Circuit which operate, hydraulically, the primary control surfaces such as ailerons, rudder, elevators and spoilers. Failure of such a circuit on most modern aircraft may lead to loss of control and so it is important to ensure that only clean fluid reaches the Powered Flying Control Units (PFCUs).

The PFCUs are made to very fine, or close, tolerances and the slightest scratch internally may create an internal leak and so make the unit unserviceable.

In such a system the Pressure Filter is fitted at the beginning of the PFCU circuit as a back up to the main, or supply, Pressure Filter.

Note in both cases the High Pressure, or Pressure Filter is fitted after the engine driven pump.

The design of High Pressure Filters vary considerably and so in this chapter only one example is shown.

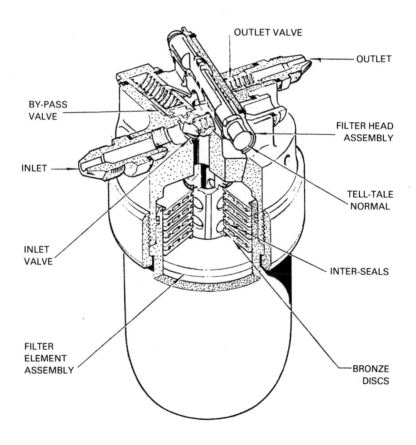

Fig.9-3. High Pressure Filter.

56

The important features of the filter are:

(a) An element capable of removing very small particles – for example 5 Microns, a further name for these filters is 'A MICRONIC FILTER'.

(b) A 'Tell Tale' indicator, i.e. a red button which protrudes when the filter element is blocked, warning that the element must be changed.

(c) If the element becomes blocked a relief valve opens in the filter allowing unfiltered fluid to by-pass the element in such an emergency.

9.3 Engine Driven or Main Hydraulic Pump

This pump provides the main hydraulic fluid flow to the various systems. The pump is normally driven by the engine via a gearbox, and is usually mounted on the engine, be it a piston, or gas turbine type of engine.

The Engine driven pump is normally one of two basic types:

(a) a fixed volume pump

or

(b) a variable volume pump

9.4 Fixed Volume Pump

This type of pump delivers a fixed quantity, or volume, of fluid to the hydraulic system at a particular speed of rotation regardless of the requirements of the system. Two main points can therefore be established with this type of pump.

(a) Fluid flow rate will vary with engine rpm. The lower the engine rpm, the lower the output, or flow rate from the pump.

(b) System pressure in a supply system fitted with this type of pump requires another component to be fitted to control the system pressure, this is normally achieved with the use of an Automatic Cut Out Valve (ACOV).

The following paragraphs describe two common types of Fixed Volume Pump that are currently fitted to aircraft.

9.5 Radial Multi/Piston Type (Fixed Volume)

Fig.9-4 illustrates such a type which consists of a drive shaft, driven by the engine, mounted in the centre of a cylinder block. The drive shaft has a cam mounted on it and during each revolution of the shaft each piston moves into and out of its cylinder once. Fluid is drawn into the pump body, and enters each cylinder, through ducting in the cylinder block, whenever the associated piston is at the bottom of its stroke. As a piston moves outwards into its cylinder, it covers the inlet port, and forces the fluid out of the top of the cylinder, past a delivery valve, to the pump outlet connection.

The pump drive shaft is mounted on needle roller bearings and is lubricated by the hydraulic fluid which flows through the pump.

Temperature control is also maintained by the fluid passing through the pump.

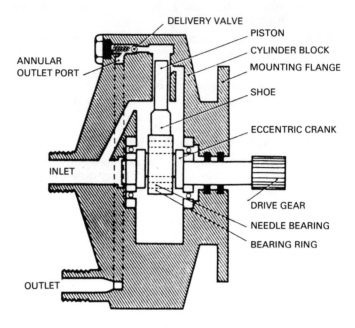

Fig.9-4. Radial Piston Pump (Fixed Volume).

9.6   Axial Piston Pump Type (Fixed Volume)

Fig.9-5 illustrates an Axial Piston Pump Type in which the pistons and cylinders are arranged radially around an eccentric crankshaft, so that when the crankshaft is rotated, a piston moves up and down in each cylinder once per revolution. Fluid is drawn into the pump body, and enters each cylinder, through ducting or drillings in the cylinder block,

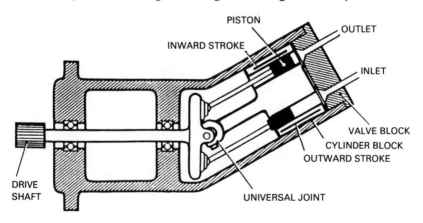

Fig.9-5. Axial Piston Pump (Fixed Volume).

whenever the associated piston is at the bottom of its stroke. As a piston moves outwards into its cylinder it covers the inlet port, and forces fluid out of the top of the cylinder, past a delivery valve, to the pump outlet connection.

Just as the Radial Multi Piston Type fixed volume pump, temperature and lubrication is controlled by the fluid passing through the pump.

Again this type of pump requires an Automatic Cut Out Valve (ACOV), or similar device, to be fitted to the system to control system pressure.

9.7 Variable Volume Pump

The Variable Volume Pumps are similar in design and construction to the Fixed Volume Pumps. Generally however, modern pumps favour a co-axial principle in that the pistons are attached to shoes which rotate against a stationary plate or yoke and a variable volume capability, and therefore.control of system pressure, can be achieved by control of the yoke angle. This type of layout is termed a Swash Plate Pump.

9.8 Swash Plate Pump (Variable Volume)

Fig.9-6 shows an example of a Swash Plate Pump. When pressure in the system is low, as would occur when a service is selected, spring pressure on the control piston turns the yoke to its maximum angle, and the pistons are at full stroke, delivering maximum output to the system. When the actuator, or jack, of the selected service reaches the end of its travel, pressure builds up until the control piston moves the yoke to the minimum stroke position; in this position the pump may be said to be at minimum stroke position, off load position or at idle position. In this position a small amount of fluid is allowed to flow through the pump to lubricate working parts, overcome internal leakage and dissipate heat.

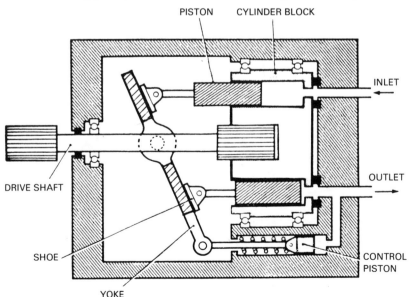

Fig.9-6. Variable Volume Swash Plate Hydraulic Pump. ·

On some pumps a solenoid operated depressurising valve is used to block delivery to the system, and to off load the pump.

9.9   Hand Pumps

Some aircraft are fitted with hand operated pumps in the supply system for one, or both, of the following purposes:

(a) for emergency use, in the event of total engine driven pump failure, for a purpose such as lowering the undercarriage.

(b) for ground servicing purposes such as pressurising the hydraulic system for testing various circuits for leaks.

Most modern hydraulic hand pumps are of a double acting type, that is to say, they provide a flow of fluid in both the up and down strokes of the piston.

9.10   Double Acting Hand Pump

Fig.9-7 shows an example of a double acting type hand pump. In basic operation as the piston moves upward in the pump cylinder, fluid is drawn into the cylinder via a non-return valve (NRV) at the inlet connection, at the same time fluid above the piston is forced through a non-return valve in the outlet connection.

As the piston moves downwards, the inlet NRV closes and the transfer NRV, located in the piston, opens, allowing hydraulic fluid to flow through the piston into the upper space above the piston. Since the volume below the piston is greater than the volume above the piston, some of the fluid will be discharged through the inlet port or connection. When pressure in the outlet line exceeds the relief valve setting, discharged fluid is bypassed back to the pump inlet creating in effect an idling circuit.

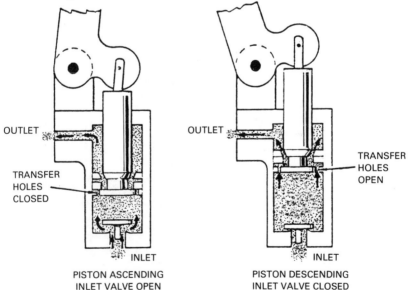

Fig.9-7. Double Acting Hydraulic Hand Pump.

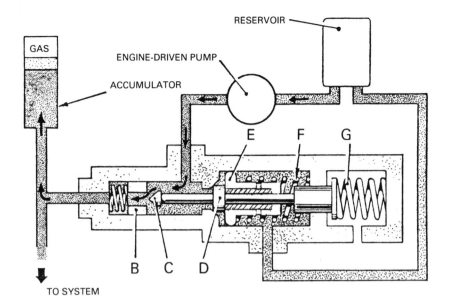

PUMP CHARGING CIRCUIT AND ACCUMULATOR

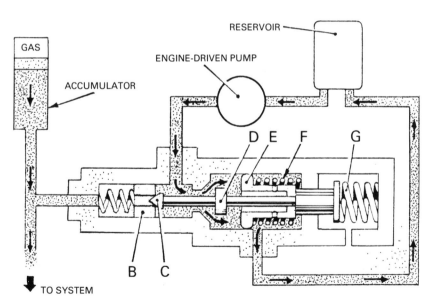

CIRCUIT AND ACCUMULATOR CHARGED

Fig.9-8. Automatic Cut Out Valve.

9.11   System Pressure Control Components

System pressure control can be divided into two specific requirement areas, firstly to control the overall system pressure, or in some cases a sub-system pressure, and secondly an emergency system to relieve excess pressure due to a fault which may arise due to a fault in the system or sub-system. The basic components and their functions are as follows:

(a)   Engine Driven Pump Pressure Control

As has been previously explained a Fixed Volume Pump has no built-in pressure control but depends on an Automatic Cut Out Valve, fitted after the pump to control system pressure.

A Variable Volume Pump however has the ability to control system pressure and generally controls that pressure to maintain 3000 psi on most modern aircraft.

(b)   Automatic Cut Out Valve (ACOV)

When a Fixed Volume Pump is fitted to the system an automatic cut out valve is fitted, usually immediately after the pump, to control system pressure, thus providing the pump with an idling circuit when no services have been selected.

To aid the automatic cut out valve in its operation it is essential to fit an accumulator immediately after the ACOV since any slight leakage through components, or from the system, would result in operation of the ACOV, and in the frequent loading and unloading of the pump. Such frequent operation of the ACOV is generally termed hydraulic hammering or chattering. Fig.9-8 illustrates the basic operation of an automatic cut out valve. When a service has been selected and the pump is delivering fluid to the system, the non-return valve, NRV, is open and equal pressure is applied to the poppet valve and piston; the force of the spring combined with the pressure on the poppet valve, is greater than the force on the piston, so the valve is closed and the return line to the reservoir is blocked. When a service is selected and has completed its travel, pressure builds up in the delivery line to the system until the force applied to the piston is sufficient to lift the poppet valve off its seat; this results in a sudden drop in pressure on the pump side of the poppet valve which rapidly opens the poppet valve and closes the NRV. Pressure in the return line drops to a low value and the load on the pump is reduced, or removed. The output from the pump is now allowed to return to the reservoir, and pressure in the system is maintained by the accumulator until a further selection is made; when pressure drops and the force on the cut out piston becomes less than the spring force, the poppet valve closes and pump output is again directed into the system.

(c)   Pressure Relief Valves

Relief valves are essentially the simplest form of pressure limiting device and may be used as separate valves or may be incorporated within other components such as selectors etc. A relief valve is frequently used as a safety device where it is set to relieve pressure, or blow off, at a pressure slightly higher than maximum system normal working pressure, and is so designed to relieve only a small quantity of fluid.

Fig.9-9 shows a simple relief valve such as that which may be fitted in most sub-systems such as the alighting gear circuit.

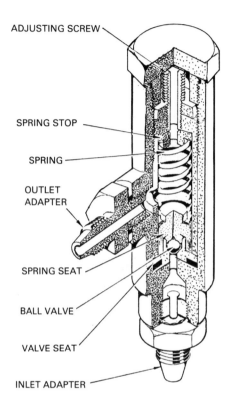

ADJUSTING SCREW

SPRING STOP

SPRING

OUTLET ADAPTER

SPRING SEAT

BALL VALVE

VALVE SEAT

INLET ADAPTER

Fig.9-9. Pressure Relief Valve.

(1)   Simple Pressure Relief Valve
This comprises a simple ball valve held against its seat by a spring. The spring is adjusted to impose a force on the ball valve so that when the maximum permitted pressure is felt on the ball it will open allowing a small amount of fluid to return to the reservoir via the return line and therefore reducing the pressure in the circuit.

(2)   Thermal Relief Valve
Generally these are similar in construction and operation to the type shown in 9.9. The Thermal Relief Valve is primarily fitted to relieve excess pressure in a system that is caused by thermal expansion of the hydraulic fluid. As such the thermal relief valve is fitted in a circuit, which when certain selections are made, becomes a 'closed circuit' and the fluid in the circuit becomes isolated under

pressure forming a hydraulic lock. Such a condition may exist when the aircraft is parked on the ground in high temperature conditions causing the fluid to expand and excess pressure to be generated. The excess pressure will be relieved by the thermal relief valve allowing only a very small amount of fluid to return to the reservoir. It is important to note the hydraulic thermal relief valve is sensitive to pressure and not temperature.

Some thermal relief valves are fitted with a restrictor prior to the ball valve to ensure they respond to pressure increase and not a sudden surge in fluid flow.

(3)   Full Flow Relief Valves
Whilst some relief valves are designed to allow only a small amount of fluid to return to the reservoir when relieving excess pressure others are designed to allow full fluid flow through them. An example of such a valve is shown in Fig.9-10. One example of the use of such a valve would be in a flap circuit where, in the event the flaps were lowered at too high an airspeed, the pressure of air on flaps would cause the fluid pressure in the hydraulic flap circuit to rise, and so, the relief valve would open allowing the fluid to flow back to return at full flow rate. This would allow the flaps to return to the fully up position preventing any damage to the flaps or the aircraft structure, and indeed, the hydraulic system.

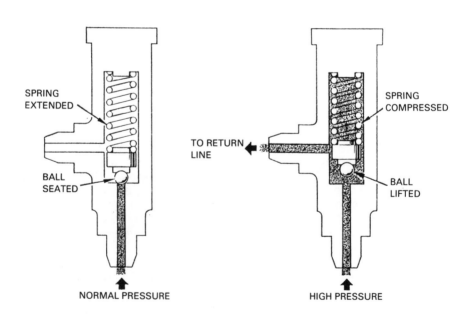

Fig.9-10. Pressure Relief Valve (Full Flow).

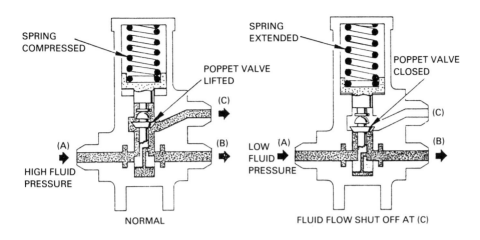

Fig.9-11. Pressure Maintaining Valve.

(d) Pressure Maintaining Valve

Pressure Maintaining Valves are essentially pressure relief valves which are designed to maintain a set value of pressure in a primary, or essential circuit, when a leakage occurs in the secondary, or non-essential circuits. For example, if a leak occurs in a non-essential service, once the system pressure has fallen to a certain value, the pressure maintaining valve will close off fluid supply to non-essential services reserving what fluid is left for essential services.

In some cases the pressure maintaining valve may be called a Priority Valve. It must be noted however that a Priority Valve, whilst performing the same basic function, achieves it in a different way. See Fig.9-11.

(e) Priority Valve

The priority valve is normally an electrically operated valve which is connected to a fluid level switch in the reservoir. In the event a leak occurs in the secondary circuits, or, anywhere in the primary system, which causes the fluid level in the reservoir to fall to a certain level, the fluid level switch operates the priority valve, closing off supply to non-essential services and reserving what fluid is left for essential services only, such as powered flying controls.

9.12   Pressure Reducing Valve

Some circuits, or sub-systems, are required to operate at a reduced pressure. An example of such a sub-system is the Wheel Brake Circuit. On most aircraft the wheel brakes are operated at pressures of 1500 psi, in such cases the pressure reducing valve will reduce the pressure from 3000 psi, or whatever the system normal working pressure is, to the pressure required. In most wheel brake circuits the pressure is reduced within the Brake Control Valve. In some circuits a separate pressure reducing valve is required, an example of which is shown in Fig.9-12.

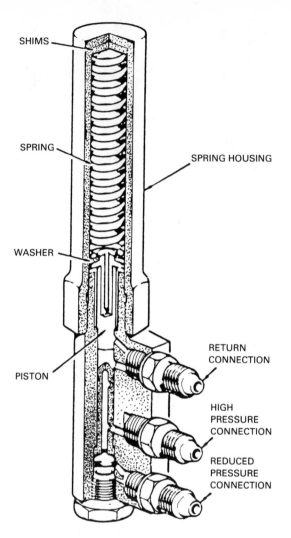

SHIMS

SPRING

SPRING HOUSING

WASHER

PISTON

RETURN
CONNECTION

HIGH
PRESSURE
CONNECTION

REDUCED
PRESSURE
CONNECTION

Fig.9-12. Pressure Reducing Valve.

The valve consists of a body and a spring housing and works on the same principle as a pressure relief valve. The piston assembly is bored part of its length and has two grooves on the outside which are drilled to allow fluid to pass into or out of the bore. The spring assembly holds the piston on its seat and is adjustable by shims (thin washers). The adjustment will vary the reduced pressure dependent on the value required. There are three connections — the return line, high pressure line and a reduced pressure line.

Operation of Reducing Valve
When the piston is seated by the spring pressure, high pressure fluid flows, via the drilling in the piston, from the high pressure line to the

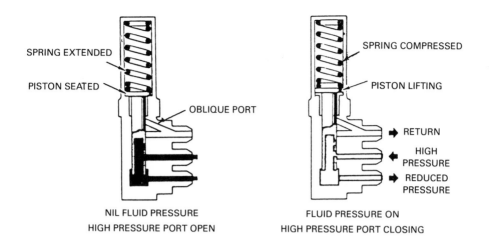

Fig.9-13. Operation of Pressure Reducing Valve.

reduced pressure line. The high pressure fluid however, acts on the piston and when the fluid pressure exceeds the spring pressure, the piston rises and closes the high pressure port, and, if the reduced pressure is increased by an external force, the piston movement continues and opens the return port to relieve the pressure.

When a reduction in pressure within the valve occurs the spring returns the piston which closes the return port, and continued movement opens the high pressure port again. Any tendency of the piston to 'chatter', i.e. a hunting movement of the piston up and down the cylinder, is damped out by the gradual closing of the oblique port of the return connection, thereby restricting the flow of fluid displaced.

9.13   Pressure or Fluid Release Valves

It is important to note the name of this valve and NOT get it confused with a Pressure Relief Valve.

The Pressure Release Valve is used to release pressure from a circuit or system, and, for example is often used to dump or release system pressure prior to checking the fluid level of the reservoir, and checking the initial, or pre-charge, or gas pressure of an accumulator.

The release valve illustrated in Fig.9-11 consists of a body containing a valve assembly of a ball and spring, and a button or plunger.

Operation

With no load on the button, fluid under pressure at the inlet connection is sealed off by the ball valve assembly, and the spindle is held clear of the ball by its spring. When the button is depressed the spindle lifts the ball off its seat and fluid can flow from the inlet connection to the outlet connection, via the side of the ball valve. When the button is released the valve automatically closes. See Fig.9-14.

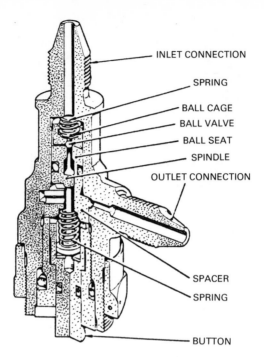

INLET CONNECTION

SPRING

BALL CAGE

BALL VALVE

BALL SEAT

SPINDLE

OUTLET CONNECTION

SPACER

SPRING

BUTTON

Fig.9-14. Fluid Release Valve.

9.14 Non-Return Valves

The non-return valve allows full flow of fluid in one direction only. An arrow is normally marked on the side of the valve body to indicate the direction of free flow. Non-return valves are used in most systems to provide various services. As was seen in the supply circuit, the non-return valve was used to prevent hand pump fluid being pumped back through the engine driven pump side of the circuit, and engine driven pump fluid passing back through the hand pump circuit.

An important feature of the non-return valve is its fitting to the inlet side of a system control valve. In this situation it provides a hydraulic lock by allowing fluid from supply to enter the circuit and preventing its return through the same pipeline, or connection. In a flap circuit this is used to provide a hydraulic lock, for example, when flaps are selected to the maximum lift position, when that position is reached the control valve moves to neutral preventing any further movement of the flaps. The non-return valve in such an instance prevents fluid from being drawn back out of the inlet connection which may be caused by cavitation as the result of the operation of another service.

Operation of Non-Return Valve
An example non-return valve is shown in Fig.9-15. Fluid entering the inlet connection forces the conical valve off its seat and passes through the centre drilling in the body. Fluid pressure applied to the outlet connection simply retains the conical valve on its seat, therefore preventing flow of fluid through the valve.

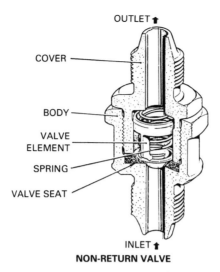

NON-RETURN VALVE

Fig.9-15. Non-Return Valve.

Note: Non-Return Valves are sometimes called 'Check Valves'.

9.15   Pressure Relay Valve

Pressure Relay Valves are a form of safety valve which are fitted in a hydraulic line to a Pressure Gauge so that in the event the gauge leaks the valve will seal off the pipeline thus preventing loss of fluid. If this should happen indication of fluid pressure will be lost. The valve incorporates a valve within its piston which is for bleeding purposes only. For the purpose of understanding its operation consider the valve to be part of the piston. System pressure will be felt on one side of the piston and is transmitted by the piston to the fluid above and then via the fluid to the gauge.

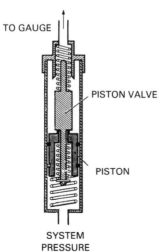

Fig.9-16. Pressure Relay Valve.

9.16   Power Pack

A Hydraulic Power Pack is a small self-contained hydraulic system which is usually designed so that it can be easily removed from the aircraft for ease of servicing. Virtually the complete system can be removed with the possible exception of the jacks, or actuators.

Such systems are normally fitted to light aircraft and helicopters. In the system shown in Fig.9-17, the pack consists of:

(a) An Electrically Driven Pump
   This provides normal system pressure by drawing fluid from the sump type reservoir. A filter is normally fitted to the pump inlet. Some packs are also provided with a hand pump for emergency use in the event of main supply pump failure.

(b) An Accumulator
   This provides initial impetus for operation of services and damps out pump pulsations.

(c) Selector
   A selector is provided to select the service operation required.

A number of packs may be fitted to provide hydraulics to operate a number of services and may be interconnected to provide emergency pressure in the event of one pump failing.

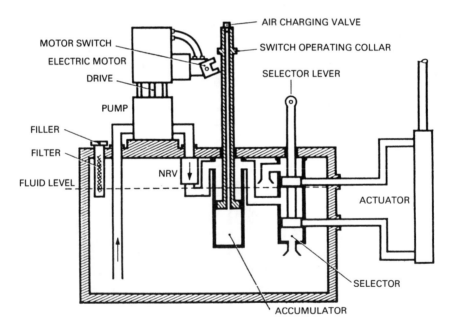

Fig.9-17. Power Pack System.

9.17   Hydraulic Motors

In some systems hydraulic motors are used to operate some services such as flaps, slats and similar devices. The hydraulic motor normally takes the form of a swash plate design and operates like a swash plate pump in reverse. Fluid is fed under pressure to the motor which then converts the fluid pressure into rotary mechanical motion. Constant speed motors normally have a flow control valve fitted at the inlet to achieve a constant flow rate and hence a constant speed.

9.18 Flow Control Valves

The designs of this type of valve are many and varied. One example has been mentioned before in the flap circuit in the form of a Throttling Valve. The flow control valve is essentially a sophisticated two way restrictor in that it provides a constant flow rate in both directions.

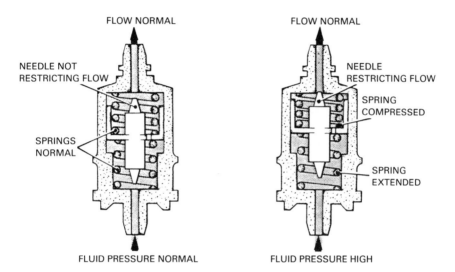

Operation. With fluid pressure normal, fluid flows through the piston ports, but an increase in the pressure or an increase in the flow to the valve, which would increase the pressure on one side of the piston moves the piston in the direction of the flow. The leading needle approaches and enters the bush and restricts the flow of fluid out of the valve. The design of the valve and strength of the springs ensure that the needles will not seat and completely shut off the flow.

Fig.9-18. Flow Control Valve.

9.19 Selector or Control Valves

Hydraulic control valves are generally either mechanically or electrically operated and vary considerably in their design. Many control valves are provided with a neutral setting in order that a hydraulic lock may be created, as in the flap circuit.

TEST YOURSELF 9
HYDRAULIC COMPONENTS

1. The stack pipe in a reservoir:
   (a) is connected to the main engine driven pump supply.
   (b) is designed to hold a reserve of fluid for the engine driven pump.
   (c) ensures a reserve of fluid for the hand pump in the event fluid level is low.
   (d) ensures the fluid is de-aerated on return.

   Ref. 9.1.

2. To compensate for variations in aircraft attitude some reservoirs are fitted with:
   (a) a stack pipe.
   (b) a flexible hose on the supply connection.
   (c) a diffuser to reduce aeration.
   (d) a system of baffles.

   Ref. 9.1.

3. Low Pressure Filters are normally fitted:
   (a) in the return line.
   (b) in the pressure supply.
   (c) in low pressure systems only.
   (d) between the reservoir and engine driven pump.

   Ref. 9.2.

4. Some High Pressure Filters are:
   (a) fitted with Tell Tale indicators to indicate element blockage.
   (b) fitted with Tell Tale indicators to indicate free flow.
   (c) fitted with Tell Tale indicators to show excess system pressure.
   (d) fitted with Tell Tale indicators to indicate useful life.

   Ref. 9.2.

5. Pressure Filters are:
   (a) normally fitted before the pump to prevent cavitation.
   (b) normally fitted after the engine driven pump.
   (c) normally fitted in the engine driven pump.
   (d) normally fitted in very high pressure circuits.

   Ref. 9.2.

6. Pressure in a Variable Volume Swash Plate Pump Supply System is controlled by:

    (a) the automatic cut-out valve.

    (b) the Yoke.

    (c) the Control Piston.

    (d) the Accumulator.

    Ref. 9.8.

7. When in the 'off load position', of a variable volume swash plate pump supply system:

    (a) all fluid is returned to the reservoir.

    (b) the pump will stop.

    (c) the ACOV will direct the fluid back to the reservoir.

    (d) some fluid will still pass through the pump.

    Ref. 9.8.

8. When a Double Acting Hand Pump is:

    (a) on the downward stroke the transfer valve is open.

    (b) on the upward stroke the transfer holes are open.

    (c) on the downward stroke the inlet valve is open.

    (d) on the upward stroke the inlet valve is closed.

    Ref. 9.10.

9. A Thermal Relief Valve is:

    (a) sensitive to pressure.

    (b) sensitive to temperature.

    (c) only used with a normal pressure relief valve.

    (d) normally used in supply circuits only.

    Ref. 9.11.

10. In order to allow flaps to be blown back to their fully up position in the event they are selected at high speed:

    (a) a thermal relief valve is fitted in the flap circuit.

    (b) a pressure relief valve is fitted in the flap circuit.

    (c) a pressure relief valve is fitted in the pump.

    (d) a thermal relief valve is fitted in the supply circuit.

    Ref. 9.11.

11. Pressure Maintaining Valves are fitted to:

    (a) relieve excess system pressure.

    (b) to protect non-essential services.

(c) to protect essential services.

(d) to protect secondary services.

Ref. 9.11.

12. In some systems in place of a pressure maintaining valve a:

(a) priority valve is fitted.

(b) pressure relief valve is fitted.

(c) thermal relief valve is fitted.

(d) sequence valve is fitted.

Ref. 9.11.

13. Chatter in a pressure reducing valve is prevented by:

(a) fitting an accumulator.

(b) fitting washers under the spring.

(c) the oblique port.

(d) a duplicated spring.

Ref. 9.12.

14. System pressure may be released by:

(a) operation of a pressure relief valve.

(b) operation of a pressure release valve.

(c) operation of the drain valves.

(d) operation of the bleed valves.

Ref. 9.13.

15. A hydraulic lock may be provided by fitting:

(a) a non-return valve to the outlet of the control valve.

(b) a pressure relief valve to the outlet of the control valve.

(c) a non-return valve to the inlet of the control valve.

(d) a non-return valve to the inlet of the jack.

Ref. 9.14.

10

SERVICING ASPECTS AND FAULT DIAGNOSIS

10.1 Introduction

It is important the pilot has an understanding of certain aspects of the servicing requirements of hydraulic systems and also a capability of diagnosing faults that may arise, together with a basic understanding of the implications of such faults.

10.2 Checking the Level of the Reservoir

At first sight this may seem a very basic task. Normally before each flight the hydraulic fluid level should be checked in the reservoir, and if required, should be topped up accordingly. The first point that must be considered is that if the fluid level is low, it should be reported to the engineer as this may be the result of a leak in the system. The following is the general procedure that must be followed when checking the fluid level:

(a) Fluid Level Indication
    The fluid level may be indicated in a number of ways:

        (i)   Sight Glass
            This takes the form of a small glass, or plastic, window mounted in the casing of the reservoir which indicates the actual fluid level. Adjacent to the window are markings which usually are marked, 'MAX', 'Normal' and 'MIN'. 'MAX' for Maximum and 'MIN' for Minimum levels.

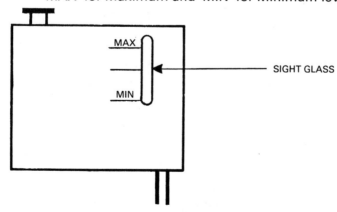

Fig. 10-1. Reservoir Sight Glass.

For safe operations the level should be between the 'MAX' or Upper mark and 'MIN' the Lower mark.

If topping up of the fluid level is required then it is normal practice to top up the level to the Upper Mark.

(ii) Cockpit Indicator

An indication of the fluid level in the hydraulic reservoir may be given in the cockpit in the form of a gauge, transmitted from a float in the reservoir, or on some modern aircraft through a visual display panel.

(b) Checking the Level

Before the actual fluid level may be checked on the reservoir, certain actions must be carried out to obtain an accurate indication. They are as follows:

(i) All Systems are in the Correct Position

This statement means that all systems, such as flaps, are in the correct position for checking the reservoir, that is to say, the flaps are in the 'Down' position. The position of some services may differ between aircraft types and so the aircraft manual must be consulted, however, as a general example flaps are normally required to be in the down position.

The position of the services is very important to the level of fluid in the reservoir due mainly to 'Jack Ram Displacement'. Other services such as speed brakes, wheel brakes and sometimes certain hydraulically operated doors must be in the correct position before any attempt to check the fluid level is carried out.

(ii) All System Pressure must be released

During the normal operation of the hydraulic system such components as hydraulic accumulators will be pressurised with system hydraulic fluid and so, in order that an accurate check of the fluid level of the reservoir can be completed such system pressure must be released and under normal operation will return to the reservoir through the common return line and therefore effectively increase the level in the reservoir. As can be seen, if the fluid level in the reservoir was topped up as a result of system pressure not being released, then the reservoir will be effectively overfilled which may result in the reservoir exploding under system operation due to excess fluid in the reservoir. Whilst protection devices are fitted to prevent such over-pressurisation of the reservoir, overfilling of the reservoir or system should be avoided.

Even with the components in the correct position and the system fluid pressure released it is still not correct to check the fluid level in the reservoir.

(iii) Check Accumulator Charge Pressures

After system pressure (fluid pressure) has been released,

the accumulator charge pressures must be checked and corrected as required. If the accumulator charge pressure is low, then it is possible that not all of the fluid has been expelled from the accumulator when system pressure was released. Again this may result in a false low fluid level indication in the reservoir.

(iv) Summary
Before checking the reservoir fluid level of an aircraft hydraulic system:

   (i)   All systems must be in the correct positions.

  (ii)   All system fluid pressure must be released.

 (iii)   All accumulator charge pressures must be correct.

10.3 Topping Up the Fluid Level of the Reservoir

If it is found necessary to top up the level of the reservoir then first ensure the correct type of hydraulic fluid is to be used. The type is as stated in the aircraft manual.

Note: On some aircraft not only must the specification of fluid be correct, but also only a specific make of brand must be used.

Hydraulic reservoirs vary considerably in design and so the procedure recommended in the aircraft manual must be followed when topping up the reservoir.

10.4 Checking for Leaks

Checking for leaks from the system is important in the event that the reservoir requires to be topped up. Whilst minor leakages may be accepted to a degree, any major topping up would indicate a major external leakage of fluid, and in such cases every effort should be made to trace the leak and rectify it. Most hydraulic fluids contain a coloured dye which assists in the process of tracing leaks, such as the red dye contained in D.T.D. 585. External leaks will be indicated by a fall in reservoir fluid level and are therefore easily noticed.

Internal leaks present a more serious problem from the point of view of detection.

An internal hydraulic leak is one which is caused by leakage of fluid past a seal or valve seat internally from one part of the hydraulic system to another. Some internal leaks are a design feature and so are intentional and therefore acceptable, other internal leaks are the result of failure of a seal or valve seat and results in reduced performance of the system. The latter type of internal leak is often hard to detect under normal operational conditions as normally it is not accompanied by a drop in hydraulic fluid level due to the fact that such fluid that leaks past seals etc., will eventually find its way back to the reservoir. A clear indication of an internal fluid leak is an increase in the temperature of the hydraulic fluid. Temperature sensors and indicators are fitted to modern hydraulic systems to enable the pilot to monitor such conditions. The temperature sensors are usually located in the reservoir, or sometimes the return line to the reservoir. The rise in temperature of the fluid due to an internal leak is caused by the diffusion of the fluid after it has passed through the leakage area, i.e. a broken seal, which causes rapied expansion, a rise in pressure, accompanied by a rise in temperature.

10.5 Priming and Bleeding

The priming of a hydraulic system is to initially fill the system with hydraulic fluid. This is usually carried out after the system has been drained of hydraulic fluid when extensive servicing has been carried out involving the removal and refitting of numerous hydraulic components. In such circumstances the system is filled with hydraulic fluid (Priming) and then has to be bled of any air that may be trapped in the system. Every effort must be made to remove all air from the system as air in a hydraulic system will have serious effects on the system performance resulting in slow and often erratic operation.

Bleeding is carried out in two primary ways:

(a) Static Bleeding
    This type of bleeding is completed by pressurising the hydraulic system and, under static conditions – that is components are stationary – air is bled from specific bleed points located in the various circuits. Such points are termed bleed nipples. It is usual to commence bleeding air from the system at the furthest and lowest point from the pump and work back towards the pump. System pressure is maintained throughout the operation normally by operation of the hand pump, and the reservoir must be kept topped up continually.

(b) Dynamic Bleeding
    This type of bleeding sometimes termed 'Venting', is completed by operating the pump and through selection of the various circuits, circulates fluid through the system taking the air, with the return fluid, back to the reservoir. The air is allowed to escape through the filler of the reservoir. In most cases it requires a combination of both static and dynamic bleeding to be used to rid the system of air.

10.6 Incorrect Fluid put into Reservoir (Fluid Contamination)

In the event that the incorrect type of fluid is used in topping up the hydraulic reservoir the complete system must be drained, flushed with cleaning fluid, seals changed as required – in most cases all seals – and then finally primed and bled.

It must be fully realised that if the incorrect fluid is used in a hydraulic system the results can be very serious. The fluid will almost certainly cause serious damage to seals, and in some cases, to protective coatings on the internal surfaces of hydraulic components.

10.7 Fault Diagnosis

The primary indicators of faults in a hydraulic system are as follows:

(a) Indicated Pressure
    A fault in a system may be indicated by a reduction in pressure, or the illumination of a pressure failure warning light, or a combination

of both. Such an indication may be caused by a leak in the system or a possible pending failure of a hydraulic pump.

(b) Operating Times

A good indication of the serviceability state of a hydraulic system is the time a service takes to complete its operating cycle. For example, an undercarriage system should take fourteen seconds to retract, it actually takes twenty-eight seconds. In this case it indicates a flow rate of the fluid which has halved, in a two pump supply circuit this would indicate that possibly one pump has failed.

(c) Temperature

A rise in hydraulic fluid temperature could possibly be an indication of an internal fluid leak.

(d) Slow Operation, Sometimes Erratic

For example, slow and/or erratic operation of the flaps when selected may indicate air in the flap circuit.

(e) Filter Blockage

The blockage of a filter element has little or no immediate effect on the operation of the system. If the filter element becomes blocked, a By-pass Valve, or Relieve Valve, will open as pressure builds up, allowing the fluid to flow through the filter body, by-passing the filter element. This does however mean the fluid is not being filtered and continued use in this mode will eventually cause damage to the system if particles of foreign matter are in the fluid.

Most modern filters are equipped with a 'Tell Tale' indicator, in the form of a red button, which indicates if the filter element is blocked and should therefore be changed. Some filters are also equipped with a cockpit indicator which warns of filter blockage.

(f) Engine Driven Pump Failure

In a two pump supply system, if one pump should fail, then the following conditions will exist:

(i) System pressure will remain the same.

(ii) Supply flow rate will be halved.

(iii) Operating times will be doubled.

(g) Low Accumulator Initial Charge Pressure

If the initial charge pressure of the air, or nitrogen, in the accumulator is low then the accumulator's ability to compensate for minor leaks or fluctuations in the system will be reduced, as a result the automatic cut out valve will cut in and out more frequently which will be indicated as rapid system pressure fluctuations. Whilst the above conditions exist for a fixed volume pump system, with an ACOV similar conditions will also exist for variable volume systems in relationship to the pump if the system accumulator has a low initial charge pressure.

(h) Checking Accumulator Charge Pressure

Before the pressure of the air or nitrogen can be checked in an accumulator, all system fluid pressure must be released. A special adaptor is then fitted to the accumulator charging valve and a lever on the adaptor is depressed to read the pressure.

Although a gauge is normally fitted on the accumulator the adaptor serves as a double check to ensure that the pressure is correct.

10.8 Seals

A wide variety of seals are used in modern aircraft hydraulic systems, the primary types in use are listed below.

(a) Static Seals

This type of seal is used to seal two static surfaces in the form of a gasket and effectively provide a seal when they are squeezed between two mating surfaces. The material from which they are manufactured is dictated by the type of fluid used in the system.

(b) Dynamic Seals

This type of seal is used between two sliding surfaces, such as the piston and cylinder of a jack or actuator, and vary in cross sectional shape and the material from which they are made.

(1) 'U' or 'V' shaped seals (sometimes termed a chevron seal). This type of ring seal with a 'U' or 'V' cross section effectively only seal in one direction.

(2) 'Square' or 'O' section ring seals effectively seal in both directions.

(3) Stiff Backing Rings

These are used with the seals mentioned in (1) and (2) when they are used in high pressure systems to provide support to the seal and increase their effective sealing ability.

(c) Seal Materials

Seals used in systems using D.T.D. 585 Red Hydraulic Fluid which is mineral based require Synthetic Rubber Seals.

Seals used in systems using vegetable, or castor based, hydraulic fluid coloured yellow, require natural rubber seals.

Seals used in systems using Skydrol fluid, coloured Blue, require Butyl Rubber seals. Skydrol is a Phosphate Ester based fluid.

Warning

Hydraulic fluids must never be mixed and only the specified type for that system must be used. In the event that the wrong type of fluid is put into a system the system must be drained, completely flushed through and new seals fitted.

TEST YOURSELF 10
SERVICING ASPECTS AND FAULT DIAGNOSIS

1. Before the level of a hydraulic reservoir can be checked:
   - (a) the system must be fully pressurised.
   - (b) all accumulators must be fully pressurised with system fluid.
   - (c) all system fluid pressure must be released.
   - (d) all fluid must be drained from the system.

   Ref. 10.2.

2. If the fluid level in the hydraulic reservoir requires to be topped up it should be:
   - (a) filled completely.
   - (b) filled to the normal position.
   - (c) filled to the minimum level.
   - (d) filled to the maximum level.

   Ref. 10.2.

3. Prior to checking the fluid level of a hydraulic reservoir:
   - (a) flaps must be fully up.
   - (b) accumulators must be fully pressurised with fluid.
   - (c) all services must be in the correct position.
   - (d) all fluid must be released from the system.

   Ref. 10.2.

4. Hydraulic Venting:
   - (a) is a form of vapourising of the fluid.
   - (b) is a form of static bleeding.
   - (c) is a form of dynamic bleeding and static bleeding.
   - (d) is the same as dynamic bleeding.

   Ref. 10.5.

5. Static bleeding involves the removal of air from the system:
   - (a) via the reservoir filler cap.
   - (b) via bleed valves in the reservoir.
   - (c) via bleed nipples in the reservoir.
   - (d) via bleed nipples situated throughout the system.

   Ref. 10.5.

6. In a two pump supply system, if one pump fails:
   (a) pressure will be halved.
   (b) flow rate will remain the same.
   (c) operating times will double.
   (d) operating times will be halved.

Ref. 10.7.

7. Before checking accumulator charge pressure:
   (a) all services must be in the correct position.
   (b) all system fluid pressure must be released.
   (c) all fluid must be drained from the system.
   (d) the system must be fully pressurised.

Ref. 10.7.

8. Slow operation of a service may be due to:
   (a) air in the system.
   (b) system pressure too high.
   (c) accumulator charge pressure too high.
   (d) operating times too high.

Ref. 10.7.

9. An internal leak in a hydraulic system will result in:
   (a) a low fluid level in the reservoir.
   (b) an increase in system temperature.
   (c) a reduction in system temperature.
   (d) a rise in reservoir fluid level.

Ref. 10.7.

10. Filter blockage in a hydraulic system will be indicated by:
    (a) a red 'Tell Tale' indicator protruding.
    (b) slow operation of all services.
    (c) operation of a 'Tell Tale' indicator in the cockpit.
    (d) erratic operation of all services.

Ref. 10.7.

11

EMERGENCY OPERATION OF HYDRAULIC SERVICES

11.1 Introduction

Emergency operation of a hydraulic system, in the event of normal supply failure, may be provided in a number of ways. The following are some of the more common methods of emergency operation that are employed in aircraft hydraulic systems at the present time. It should be noted that any one aircraft may adopt a number of emergency operating methods within its hydraulic systems.

11.2 Hand Pump

In the event that the engine driven hydraulic pump fails, on some aircraft with relatively small hydraulic systems, a hand operated pump may be provided to operate certain services. This is not possible on all aircraft types. On aircraft with very large hydraulic systems, and large volume hydraulic jacks, or actuators, a hand pump would be totally inadequate.

When hand pumps are used for emergency use the hydraulic reservoir has a stack-, or stand-pipe fitted in the bottom. The normal, or engine driven pump obtains its supply of hydraulic fluid from the base of the stack-pipe. This is illustrated in Fig.11-1. As can be seen, should a leak occur in the system whch causes the fluid level to fall in the reservoir, it will only fall as far as the top of the stack-pipe. The fluid that now remains in the reservoir can only be provided by the hydraulic hand pump, in other words the hand pump may be provided with its own reserve of emergency fluid.

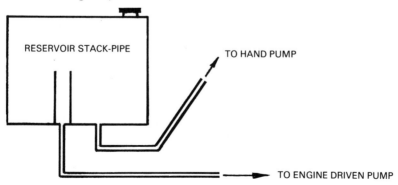

RESERVOIR STACK-PIPE

TO HAND PUMP

TO ENGINE DRIVEN PUMP

Fig.11-1. Emergency Hand Pump Connections.

On most large aircraft the hand pump is connected to the hydraulic system for servicing purposes only, and is often located in such a way that it cannot be operated in flight.

11.3 Duplicated Systems

Hydraulic supply systems on modern aircraft are normally duplicated at least, and on some aircraft may be triplicated or more. In the case of a duplicated system, in the event one pump should fail the remaining pump will continue to supply the hydraulic circuits with fluid under pressure. Fig.11-2 shows an example of a duplicated supply system.

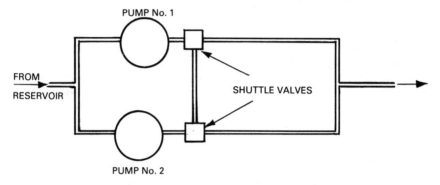

Fig.11-2. A Duplicated Hydraulic Supply System.

In such a system a shuttle valve may be provided which in the event one pump fails will close off the supply line from the unserviceable pump thus preventing any loss of fluid, or fluid pressure. In this arrangement Number Two Pump is being used as a standby pump. In this case only the pumps are really being duplicated.

In other systems the entire supply system is duplicated.

See Figure 11-3.

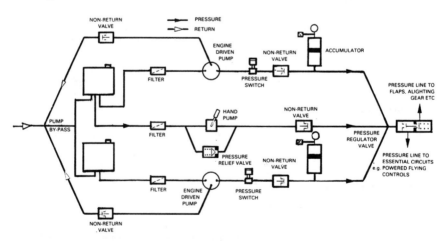

Fig.11-3. Completely Duplicated Supply.

In a fully duplicated supply system, in the event one pump fails, the following will result:

(a) System pressure will remain the same.

(b) Fluid flow rate will be halved.

(c) Operating times will double.

In some very large aircraft the systems may be Triplicated, or Quadruplicated. In such systems, or sub-systems, a code letter, number or colour may be given to each individual system or sub-system for identification purposes. For example, a given pump and its associated components may be called Number One system, or Yellow system. In such cases the pipelines may also be coded for that particular system with small bands of tape at intervals along its length, with this system leaks from a particular hydraulic system can be more easily traced. In large civil aircraft duplicated pumps are equipped with individual reservoir supply, that is, an independent reservoir supplies each individual pump, this ensures that in the event a leak, or fault occurs with a particular reservoir supply can still be maintained.

Some essential services such as powered flying controls are normally supplied from two independent sources, such as yellow and green systems, and so in the event of one system failing the other will continue to maintain supply.

On such services as the powered flying controls of the jacks, or actuator, are also duplicated to ensure control of the aircraft can be maintained even though one hydraulic system and one actuator have failed.

Fig.11-4 shows an example of duplication of powered flying controls.

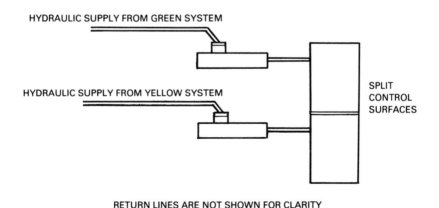

HYDRAULIC SUPPLY FROM GREEN SYSTEM

HYDRAULIC SUPPLY FROM YELLOW SYSTEM

SPLIT CONTROL SURFACES

RETURN LINES ARE NOT SHOWN FOR CLARITY

Fig.11-4. Duplication of Powered Flying Controls.

11.4 Accumulators

Accumulators may be used as a source of emergency hydraulic fluid under pressure. Due to the limited quantity of fluid that may be stored in this way they generally have very limited application.

A common circuit in which the accumulator is used as a source of emergency fluid stored under pressure is the Wheel Brake Circuit. It is installed in such a way that in the event of supply system failure, the accumulator holds sufficient fluid under pressure to operate the brakes for at least one full landing run, plus a reserve. To achieve this the wheel brake accumulators tend to be of large capacity, or there is more than one accumulator fitted to the circuit. Fig.11-5 shows an example of the wheel brake system accumulator installation.

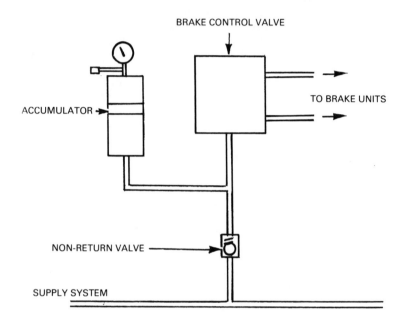

Fig.11-5. Wheel Brake Accumulator Installation.

11.5 Emergency Air Systems

Whilst essential systems such as Powered Flying Controls require an emergency fluid supply, other services, such as the undercarriage circuit, may be operated by the use of compressed air, or nitrogen, which is stored, until required for use, in storage cylinders within the airframe. By using such a system, as opposed to the use of a fully duplicated system, a considerable amount of cost and weight can be saved.

Normally, on large aircraft such systems as undercarriage, speed brakes, door operation, flaps down, and many minor services may in an emergency be operated by an emergency air, or nitrogen system.

Fig.11-6 gives a breakdown of some of the emergency systems that may be used, and in particular emergency air.

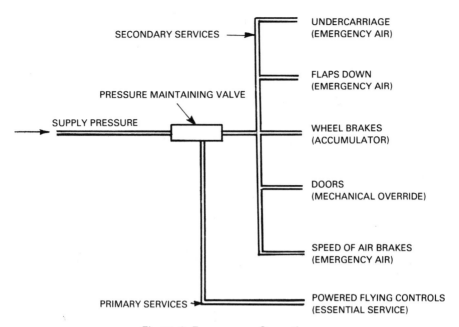

Fig.11-6. Emergency Operations.

An example of a typical emergency air supply system is shown in Fig.11-7.

In this type of system, in the event of main hydraulic supply system failure on selection of an Air Release Valve compressed air is introduced into the down line of the service to be operated. The compressed air on being released from the cylinder by the air release valve enters the down line via a shuttle valve. The compressed air causes a piston within

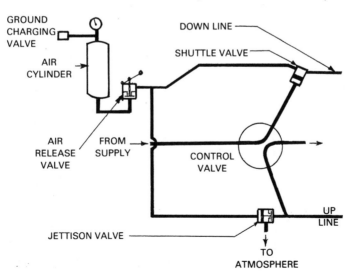

Fig.11-7. Emergency Air System.

the shuttle valve to move thereby closing the pipeline to the control valve. The compressed air then flows through the down line and with the fluid already in the pipeline creates a force great enough to operate the jack, or actuator.

The hydraulic fluid trapped in the up line will build up pressure restricting the effectiveness of the compressed air in operating the service in an emergency. To reduce this effect, on some systems, a fluid jettison valve is fitted. The fluid jettison valve is activated by the compressed air when the air release valve is operated, and so as pressure in the up line builds up the fluid jettison valve opens allowing the fluid to escape to atmosphere. In some systems the fluid jettison valve opens and returns the fluid to the reservoir.

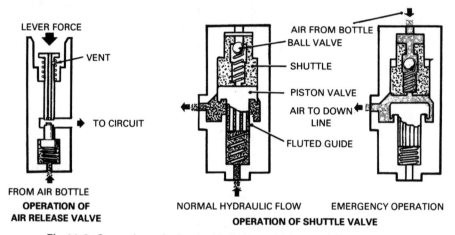

Fig.11-8. Operation of a basic Air Release Valve and Shuttle Valve.

Fig.11-9 illustrates a basic Fluid Jettison Valve.

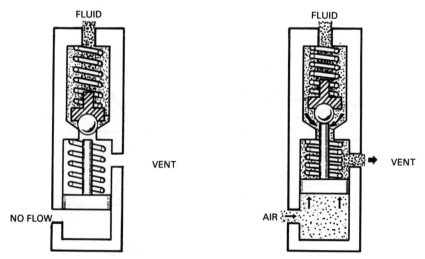

Fig.11-9. Fluid Jettison Valve.

11.6   Ram Air Turbine

Ram Air Turbine Units are used on many modern aircraft as a means to drive certain components in an emergency. In this case the Ram Air Turbine (RAT) is used to drive an emergency hyraulic pump.

When the hydraulic supply system fails the RAT automatically lowers into the airflow under the wing, or fuselage, and a small propeller, or turbine, driven by the airflow, drives an emergency hydraulic pump.

Fig.11-10 shows a simple example of a RAT.

Fig.11-10. Ram Air Turbine.

TEST YOURSELF 11
EMERGENCY OPERATION OF HYDRAULIC SERVICES

1. In an emergency system, the hand pump is sometimes provided with an emergency supply of fluid by:
   - (a) a standby reservoir.
   - (b) an accumulator.
   - (c) a stack-pipe in the base of the reservoir.
   - (d) a stack-pipe in the base of the accumulator.

   Ref. 11.2.

2. Emergency application of the wheel brakes is normally provided by:
   - (a) compressed air stored in a cylinder.
   - (b) fluid stored in an accumulator.
   - (c) fluid stored in a standby reservoir.
   - (d) a Ram Air Turbine.

   Ref. 11.4.

3. Emergency operation of the undercarriage when all supply system pressure has failed is provided by:
   - (a) an accumulator.
   - (b) a stack-pipe in the reservoir.
   - (c) a Ram Air Turbine.
   - (d) the introduction of compressed air.

   Ref. 11.5.

4. The shuttle valve of an emergency air system in an undercarriage circuit is:
   - (a) situated in the undercarriage up line.
   - (b) situated in the undercarriage down line.
   - (c) activated by the undercarriage control valve.
   - (d) activated by the jettison valve.

   Ref. 11.5.

5. A typical essential service is:
   - (a) the undercarriage circuit.
   - (b) the flap circuit.
   - (c) the wheel brake circuit.
   - (d) the PFCUs.

   Ref. 11.3.

TEST YOURSELF
FINAL PRACTICE QUESTIONS

1. D.T.D. 585 Hydraulic Fluid is:
   - (a) coloured red and requires natural rubber seals.
   - (b) yellow and requires natural rubber seals.
   - (c) blue and requires synthetic rubber seals.
   - (d) red and requires synthetic rubber seals.

   Ref. 1.4.

2. Force in a hydraulic system is:
   - (a) pressure per unit area.
   - (b) pressure divided by area.
   - (c) pressure times area.
   - (d) pressure times velocity.

   Ref. 1.6.

3. Aircraft hydraulic hand pumps are normally:
   - (a) of a single action design.
   - (b) electrically actuated.
   - (c) fitted in series with the engine driven pump.
   - (d) double acting.

   Ref. 2.2.

4. The return line from the variable volume pump to the reservoir:
   - (a) returns full flow to the reservoir when the pump is at idle.
   - (b) returns fluid to the reservoir to compensate for temperature increase.
   - (c) allows fluid to flow to the reservoir due to excess system pressure.
   - (d) allows fluid to flow from the reservoir to compensate for cavitation.

   Ref. 3.4.

5. When an ACOV is fitted to the supply circuit:
   - (a) the accumulator is fitted immediately after the pump.
   - (b) the accumulator is fitted immediately after the ACOV.
   - (c) the accumulator is not required.
   - (d) the accumulator is fitted just prior to the ACOV.

   Ref. 3.4.

6. An accumulator may:
   (a) provide initial impetus when a service is selected.
   (b) be used only in an emergency in a supply circuit.
   (c) be used only when cavitation exists in a circuit.
   (d) be used to compensate for excess pressure in a circuit.

   Ref. 3.4.

7. The warning of hydraulic system pressure failure is given by:
   (a) a warning light which illuminates when pressure reaches zero.
   (b) a warning light which illuminates when pressure drops to a certain value.
   (c) a warning light which extinguishes when pressure reaches zero.
   (d) a warning light which extinguishes when pressure drops below a certain value.

   Ref. 3.3.

8. Hydraulic hammering may be due to:
   (a) accumulator air pressure low.
   (b) accumulator fluid pressure low.
   (c) total failure of the ACOV.
   (d) low reservoir fluid level.

   Ref. 3.4.

9. Emergency wheel brakes are operated by:
   (a) emergency air.
   (b) emergency nitrogen.
   (c) accumulators.
   (d) emergency electrical operation.

   Ref. 3.6.

10. An example of a Primary Hydraulic Service:
    (a) is PFCUs.
    (b) is the undercarriage.
    (c) is the flaps.
    (d) is the speed brakes.

    Ref. 3.6.

11. The selector of the flap circuit normally:
    (a) enables a closed circuit to be created.
    (b) has a built in relief valve.

(c) has a thermal relief valve within its assembly.

(d) prevents a hydraulic lock occurring in the system.

Ref. 4.2.

12. A Two-Way Restrictor may be fitted to a flap circuit to:
    (a) prevent cavitation in the down line when flaps are selected.
    (b) prevent cavitation in the up line when flaps are selected.
    (c) provide slow smooth operation of the flaps.
    (d) prevent interference between services.

Ref. 4.4.

13. In the flap up line, excessive pressure due to thermal expansion is:
    (a) relieved by the thermal relief valve.
    (b) relieved by the pressure relief valve.
    (c) relieved by the selector.
    (d) compensated for by the accumulator.

Ref. 4.5.

14. In a hydraulic system in which a Pressure Relief Valve, and Thermal Relief Valve are fitted:
    (a) the pressure relief valve will open at the lowest pressure.
    (b) the thermal relief valve will open at the lowest pressure.
    (c) both valves will open at the same pressure.
    (d) both valves would not be fitted to the same circuit.

Ref. 4.5.

15. In flap systems on some types of aircraft, flaps are prevented from being lowered at too high an airspeed by:
    (a) the thermal relief valve.
    (b) the selector.
    (c) the two-way restrictor.
    (d) the pressure relief valve.

Ref. 4.6.

16. Flap Jacks are normally:
    (a) of equal area piston type.
    (b) of equal pressure type.
    (c) of a differential area type.
    (d) of a single ram displacement type.

Ref. 4.7.

17. Hydraulic reservoirs are normally positioned above the level of the system to provide:
    (a) a reserve of pressure should the pump fail.
    (b) a head of pressure to prevent cavitation in the reservoir.
    (c) a head of pressure to prevent cavitation at the pump.
    (d) ease of servicing.

18. High Pressure Filters are normally:
    (a) fitted between the reservoir and pump.
    (b) fitted in the return line.
    (c) fitted within the pump.
    (d) fitted after the pump.

19. An indication of the element of a high pressure filter being blocked will be:
    (a) a loss of system pressure.
    (b) a reduction of system pressure.
    (c) a tell tale indicator protruding.
    (d) an audible warning being given in the cockpit.

20. Additional protection by fitting 'Micronic Filters' is sometimes given to:
    (a) the undercarriage circuit.
    (b) the wheelbrake circuit.
    (c) the flap circuit.
    (d) the powered flying control circuit.

21. When a fixed volume pump is fitted to a hydraulic system, system pressure is:
    (a) controlled by a relief valve in the pump.
    (b) controlled by an ACOV.
    (c) controlled by a pressure maintaining valve.
    (d) controlled by an accumulator.

22. The pressure of a variable volume swash plate pump is controlled by:
    (a) the ACOV.
    (b) a pressure relief valve in the pump.

(c) a pressure relief valve after the pump.

(d) a control piston within the pump.

Ref. 9.8.

23. When the engine is shut down, the swash plate pump will:
    (a) remain at the same stroke position.
    (b) move to the off stroke position.
    (c) move to the minimum stroke position.
    (d) move to the on stroke position.

Ref. 9.8.

24. In the off load position the swash plate variable volume pump:
    (a) stops all fluid flowing.
    (b) directs all fluid back to return.
    (c) allows a small quantity of fluid through the pump.
    (d) allows full flow through the pump.

Ref. 9.8.

25. Most aircraft hydraulic systems are fitted with:
    (a) single acting hand pumps.
    (b) double acting hand pumps.
    (c) double cylinder hand pumps.
    (d) four cylinder hand pumps.

Ref. 9.10.

26. A pressure relief valve is normally set to relieve pressure at:
    (a) the same pressure as the engine driven pump.
    (b) a pressure slightly higher than the ACOV.
    (c) a pressure slightly less than the ACOV.
    (d) a pressure equal to the ACOV outlet.

Ref. 9.11.

27. A thermal relief valve is designed to be:
    (a) sensitive to temperature.
    (b) sensitive to volume change.
    (c) sensitive to pressure.
    (d) sensitive to temperature and pressure.

Ref. 9.11.

28. By fitting a restrictor pack to a thermal relief valve the valve will open:
    (a) at a lower pressure.

(b)   primarily due to pressure change.

(c)   at a higher pressure.

(d)   to allow fluid surge to the return.

Ref. 9.11.

29. Thermal relief valves:
   (a)   are normally fitted in low pressure circuits.
   (b)   are normally fitted in closed circuits.
   (c)   are normally fitted in suction lines.
   (d)   are normally fitted in parallel with pressure relief valves.

Ref. 9.11.

30. Pressure maintaining valves are normally fitted:
   (a)   after the supply circuit.
   (b)   in the supply circuit.
   (c)   in the essential circuit.
   (d)   in the non-essential circuit.

Ref. 9.11.

31. To prevent chattering of the pressure reducing valve:
   (a)   a damper spring is fitted to the valve.
   (b)   an accumulator is fitted with the valve.
   (c)   a pressure relief valve is fitted with the valve.
   (d)   an oblique port is fitted in the valve.

Ref. 9.12.

32. Pressure reducing valves are normally fitted in such systems as:
   (a)   the undercarriage circuit.
   (b)   the wheel brake circuit.
   (c)   the flap circuit.
   (d)   the supply circuit.

Ref. 9.12.

33. A pressure release valve may be used to:
   (a)   release all fluid from the system.
   (b)   release all pressure from the system.
   (c)   relieve excess pressure in an accumulator.
   (d)   release air pressure in an accumulator.

Ref. 9.13.

34. Non-return valves may be fitted just prior to a system control valve to:
    (a) prevent a hydraulic lock forming.
    (b) permit a hydraulic lock without interference.
    (c) prevent cavitation in the closed circuit.
    (d) permit cavitation in the closed circuit.
                                                        Ref. 9.13.

35. Non-return valves are sometimes called:
    (a) one way valves.
    (b) check valves.
    (c) no entry valves.
    (d) one way check valves.
                                                        Ref. 9.13.

36. The sequence of undercarriage and undercarriage door operation is controlled by the:
    (a) undercarriage control valve.
    (b) mechanical sequence valves.
    (c) sequence valve (hydraulic) valves.
    (d) regulator valves.
                                                        Ref. 5.2.

37. In an undercarriage circuit, excess pressure due to high temperature is normally relieved by:
    (a) the sequence valve hydraulic valves.
    (b) the pressure regulator valves.
    (c) the thermal relief valves.
    (d) the pressure relief valves.
                                                        Ref. 5.3.

38. Cavitation is prevented in the down line of the undercarriage circuit by:
    (a) a one way restrictor.
    (b) a check valve.
    (c) a sequence valve.
    (d) a regulator valve.
                                                        Ref. 5.3.

39. The undercarriage leg is prevented from drooping when the door is closing by the:
    (a) sequence valve.
    (b) one way restrictor.

(c) check valve.

(d) pressure regulator valve special.

Ref. 5.4.

40. The one way restrictor in the undercarriage circuit is fitted in the:
  (a) control valve.
  (b) down line.
  (c) pressure line.
  (d) up line.

Ref. 5.3.

41. When undercarriage 'Down' selection is made, the undercarriage leg:
  (a) is prevented from moving by the mechanical sequence valve.
  (b) is prevented from moving by the sequence valve hydraulic.
  (c) is prevented from moving by the check valve.
  (d) is prevented from moving by the one way restrictor.

Ref. 5.3.

42. The wheel brake accumulator is situated:
  (a) after the brake control valve.
  (b) in the supply circuit.
  (c) in the brake control valve.
  (d) before the brake control valve.

Ref. 6.3.

43. Emergency operation of the wheel brakes in the event of system supply failure is provided by:
  (a) mechanical operation.
  (b) emergency air.
  (c) stored accumulator pressure.
  (d) emergency nitrogen.

Ref. 6.3.

44. Brake system fluid pressure is normally:
  (a) increased by the brake control valve.
  (b) reduced by the brake control valve.
  (c) reduced in the supply line.
  (d) increased in the supply line.

Ref. 6.4.

45. In a wheel brake circuit:
    (a) return fluid returns via the control valve.
    (b) fluid returns via a separate return line.
    (c) a return line is not required.
    (d) a return line is fitted in the main supply.

    Ref. 6.4.

46. In a fully duplicated two pump supply system, if one pump fails:
    (a) pressure will halve.
    (b) operating times will remain the same.
    (c) flow rate will halve.
    (d) flow rate will remain the same.

    Ref. 11.3.

47. In an emergency undercarriage systems may be operated by:
    (a) emergency air.
    (b) an accumulator.
    (c) an electrical override system.
    (d) free fall.

    Ref. 11.5.

48. In an emergency, flaps may be lowered by:
    (a) an accumulator.
    (b) free fall.
    (c) a mechanical override system.
    (d) emergency air.

    Ref. 11.5.

49. In an emergency wheel brakes are normally operated by:
    (a) a mechanical override system.
    (b) an air driven pump.
    (c) an accumulator in the brake circuit.
    (d) an accumulator in the supply circuit.

    Ref. 11.5.

50. In an emergency air system, the air is supplied from:
    (a) ram air.
    (b) a compressor.
    (c) air stored in a cylinder.
    (d) air in an accumulator.

    Ref. 11.5.

51. In an undercarriage emergency air system the fluid jettison valve is normally opened by:
    (a) selection in the cockpit.
    (b) a mechanical linkage from the shuttle valve.
    (c) air from the air release valve.
    (d) air direct from the cylinder.

    Ref. 11.5.

52. In an undercarriage emergency air system the fluid jettison valve is normally situated in the:
    (a) return line.
    (b) up line.
    (c) down line.
    (d) air supply line.

    Ref. 11.5.

53. The cylinder in an emergency air system is normally charged:
    (a) in flight by a compressor.
    (b) in flight by ram air.
    (c) in flight by the compressor stage of the gas turbine.
    (d) on the ground through a charging valve.

    Ref. 11.5.

54. A RAT is:
    (a) a rotary action intensifier.
    (b) a rotary action turbine.
    (c) a ram air turbine.
    (d) a rotary air turbine.

    Ref. 11.6.

55. A RAT may be used to:
    (a) drive an emergency hydraulic pump.
    (b) drive an emergency compressor for the hydraulic system.
    (c) provide cooling air for the pumps.
    (d) provide emergency electrics for the hydraulic system.

    Ref. 11.6.

56. Prior to checking the fluid level of a hydraulic reservoir:
    (a) all accumulator air pressure must be released.
    (b) all accumulator fluid pressure must be at a maximum.
    (c) system pressure must be normal.
    (d) all fluid pressure must be released.

    Ref. 10.2.

57. Prior to checking the charge pressure of an accumulator:
    (a) all fluid pressure must be released.
    (b) all fluid must be released.
    (c) all system pressures must be at maximum.
    (d) all services must be in the fully up position.

Ref. 10.2.

58. Static Bleeding of a hydraulic system is achieved by:
    (a) operating systems and circulating the air back to the reservoir.
    (b) operating services and releasing air through release valves.
    (c) pressurising the system and releasing air through bleed valves.
    (d) pressurising the system and releasing air through pipe connections.

Ref. 10.5.

59. Indicated rapid system pressure fluctuations may be due to:
    (a) low accumulator fluid pressure.
    (b) high accumulator fluid pressure.
    (c) low accumulator charge pressure.
    (d) no system fluid pressure.

Ref. 10.7.

60. Slow operation of the flaps when selected down may be the result of:
    (a) system pressure too high.
    (b) accumulator charge pressure too high.
    (c) air in the flap circuit.
    (d) airspeed too high.

Ref. 10.7.